Painful Gifts

C.C. —

I have been deeply spiritually moved as your son & I have journeyed together over these past two years. It is my prayer that you hear God speak as you read Painful Gifts.

May God Bless.

Dewey

Painful Gifts

The Promise of Hope

DEWEY GREENE

Providence House Publishers
PROVIDENCE PUBLISHING CORPORATION
FRANKLIN, TENNESSEE

Printed in the United States of America

07   06   05   04   03   1   2   3   4   5

Library of Congress Control Number: 2003112895

ISBN: 1-57736-316-7

Cover design by Kelly Bainbridge

Cover photo and author photo by Randy Flagg

All scripture quotations are taken from the HOLY BIBLE, NEW INTERNATIONAL VERSION®. Copyright © 1973, 1978, 1984 by International Bible Society. Used by permission of Zondervan Publishing House.

For more information on Dewey Greene's ministry, see www. painfulgifts.com

PROVIDENCE HOUSE PUBLISHERS
an imprint of
Providence Publishing Corporation
238 Seaboard Lane • Franklin, Tennessee 37067
www.providence-publishing.com
800-321-5692

•

To our children
Staci, Dustin, Amber, Dana, and Megan.

With innocent hearts,
you traveled the journey with us
and God protected each of you.
May we never forget.

We love you,
Mom and Dad

and

To
John Waid, Ph.D.

From the very depths of our souls,
we thank you for "standing in the gap"
for us . . . for never giving up
(Ezek. 22:30).

Dewey and Jeannie

Contents

Foreword

Painful Gifts is one man's story, but to some degree or another, it is a story about all of us. To ascribe gifts to pain seems at first antithetical to most of us—gifts are usually associated with appreciation, reward, recognition, or achievement. But as Dewey Greene wisely reminds us, pain is always the antecedent to a gift. There is always some cost involved: the higher the cost, the greater the gift. There can be no greater gift than to know God's love for us through His Gift, and to experience His love, grace, and forgiveness.

This is a story of courage. Spiritual growth is painful, and only those courageous enough to suffer pain will ever experience the joy of intimacy with God and others. Dewey Greene's story could have remained private, only known to those involved. But, by courageously telling his story, he challenges all of us to confront the truths about ourselves. If we commit to this challenge, life will never be the same for us or for those we love; for by such commitment, we will receive the gifts of pain.

John Waid, Ph.D.

The Certainty of Pain, The Promise of Hope

I walked through the door of the corner coffee shop as they opened at 6:00 A.M. on Saturday morning. I was right on schedule . . . they unlocked the doors and I walked in. It was just like every other morning, or so I thought. I had no reason to imagine otherwise. However, as the sun crept above the treetops and darkness gave way to light, the written word would explode in virtual silence on the back of a small piece of cash register tape.

As I stepped inside, I saw Jamie, the store manager, standing behind the counter. Jamie, a thirty-something-year-old rock star look-a-like, with multiple ear piercings and dark brown spiked hair, is a great guy and a barrel of fun. His intelligence and wealth of knowledge are camouflaged by his outward appearance, and he seems to like it that way. As I walked in his direction, I said, "Jamie, I am writing a book and you are in it." In his customary flamboyant style, he laughed loudly and asked, "What part do I play?" We did our normal cut-up routine, then I got my standard cup of mild coffee and sat down at the same small round table as always, to spend time in God's Word.

A few minutes later, Jamie asked, "So what's your book about?" I went over to the counter and chatted briefly with him about the title and the concept of *Painful Gifts*. I returned to my chair and sat down, my back facing the bar, with the exterior glass wall on my immediate left.

An attractive young woman working behind the counter who had silently observed my conversation with Jamie spoke to me and said, "I admire your dedication." I stood, turned around, took two steps to the counter, and thanked her. I recognized her face as a regular coffee shop employee, but I did not know her name. I had never met her. Our conversation was brief and polite. I retraced my steps, sat down, and began to read my Bible.

An hour and a half later, I was deeply engaged in conversation with a friend, and the coffee shop was bustling with activity. Someone tapped my right shoulder, and I turned around to see the same young woman who had spoken to me earlier. She leaned down and whispered, "I would like to talk to you for ten minutes before you leave." I said, "Sure." A few minutes later, I went to the counter and told her I was available. She looked directly into my eyes and handed me a note, saying, "I wrote it down." She smiled hesitantly.

I took her note, written on a small piece of cash register tape, folded twice. I sat down and read it immediately. These were her exact words:

Painful Gifts? What about just PAIN!?!
I found out very recently I'm about 6–7 weeks along

in the process of having a baby.
I refuse to use the "p" word.
And I'm scared to death.
Nobody (except my Dr. & one friend) knows—
especially here!
I'd like to keep it that way, but wouldn't mind your prayers.
Thanks.

She felt "*pain*!?!" and she was "*scared to death.*" Struggling desperately, with no one to reach out to for help, she threw a lifeline into the darkness, asking for "*prayers,*" searching for hope. I did not know her name, but I felt her pain, her heart. This nicely dressed young woman, her long blonde hair neatly pulled back, displayed no outward indication of pain; yet, she was inwardly devastated. Unable to spend time with her to listen to her story, I went to my truck and returned with a rough draft of this book. At that moment, it was all that I could do. I wrote my cell phone number and my e-mail address on the front page of the text, and gave it to her. She smiled graciously and thanked me. A few minutes later, I left.

Two days later, I received my first e-mail from her. She told me her story, sharing her heart openly. She grew up in Virginia, an only child in the home of a Baptist minister. She walked the straight and narrow path, the "perfect" child. She became a Christian at a very young age, led a friend to the Lord when she was only ten years old, and championed the "True Love Waits" program at her church. She excelled at softball in high school. Number 25, the all-star pitcher, became all-region, all-district, all-state, all-everything. Her accomplishments earned her a college athletic scholarship and she headed for the big time, committed to her spiritual journey.

On the road to success, however, she had taken a wrong turn, and her world had become dark—very dark. She shared the heartbreaking details with me. The girl who had done everything "right" had been devastated by her mistakes, and now she was going under. Suddenly, and without warning, her deep spiritual heritage was not enough. She felt no hope. She signed her name, "Tracie."

Her subsequent e-mails to me spoke of fear, of "judgmental, legalistic, super-holy friends" who left her "crying under her sheets at night . . . her heart hurting." She wrote, "Please pray." With mounting personal struggles and financial problems at her doorstep, she had concluded that abortion seemed to be the only reasonable option.

Tracie was paralyzed . . . suddenly emotionally disconnected from friends and family, fearful for the security of her job, and hurting—pain had suffocated her heart. In the weeks ahead, when I spoke of hope, she would stare deeply into my eyes, grasping for something to hold onto. Her mind searched, wanting to believe, but her heart would fail her.

Pain, without hope, has a paralyzing effect
on the body, the mind, and the soul.

In the words of King Solomon in the thirteenth chapter of Proverbs, "Hope deferred makes the heart sick." That is precisely where Tracie was . . . heartsick.

As I share her story, I recall the distant uncertain look in her sky-blue eyes, her youthful innocence lost in confusion. I remember her forced smile, searching my face for acceptance, fearful of rejection. I felt her pain then. I can feel it now.

We have all been there, and we have all seen family and friends suffer. We read her words and we understand. Her world is our world; her story is our story. It is not difficult for me to recall recent tragedies of life that have occurred with close personal friends . . . divorce, bankruptcy, and teenage pregnancies. You can just as easily make your own list. With family financial pressures mounting, marital distress at an all-time high, the challenges of parenting ever increasing, and the certainty of death in our very midst, we are constantly facing difficult challenges . . . and often, we, like Tracie, are unprepared and overwhelmed.

Life is difficult. Pain is a universal language; it needs no interpreter. It is not a respecter of persons. Pain gives no consideration to race, creed, or color. It mocks the wealthy and famous; it suffocates the oppressed. It knows no restrictions, no limits, and no boundaries. It penetrates all barriers. There is no mountain high enough, no army large enough, and no church family spiritually deep enough to protect against—to prevent—its swift hand. It lurks in the shadows, never sleeping. It touches me, and it touches you.

Life's emotional atomic bombs do not come with advance notice. There are no warning sirens. That which we have depended on, treasured, and considered to be a certainty in life can disappear in a single heartbeat. Smoke-filled clouds billowing across the New York City skyline on September 11, 2001, and the heavens raining down thousands of pieces of the space shuttle Columbia across the southwest have removed all naïveté from our hearts. Innocence has disappeared with suddenness in our hearts, in our homes, and across our nation.

Unfortunately, life does not naturally equip us, and it is impossible to prepare for such unforeseen tragedy. Such survival tactics cannot be taught nor practiced. It is impossible to imagine, to anticipate, or to comprehend death and devastation until it has engulfed us. We find ourselves emotionally drowning. With no life-line, we feel as if we are going under for the third and final time. In that moment, the first explosive moment, nothing—and I mean nothing—gives comfort.

We scream out against God and, if we are open and honest, we often question the very existence of our faith. Sudden death and paralyzing devastation physically and emotionally bring us to our knees. Our panic-stricken hearts bleed weakness. No one is immune.

Friends of mine, godly men and women, have cried out, "I hate God," "I don't think I want to be a Christian anymore," and, "Is all this that we have taught and believed really true?" Blind-sided, we are crippled. We grope in life's darkness, in search of hope.

This book will paint a vivid picture of pain and darkness, but the heart of this story is hope. It is a book of tragedy, long-suffering, seeking, and rejoicing. It is a book about truth, about picking up the shattered pieces of life, about finding hope as an anchor for the soul, firm and secure. It is about surviving.

The certainty of hope is God's promise to us. On this journey—from life's paralyzing pain to the promise of hope—I will open my heart and share our family's story. We, too, experienced the night-marish impact of pain and suffering. We stumbled in darkness for years, and survived to catch a glimpse of God's promise of hope.

The journey begins in 1990 in East Texas. . . .

CHAPTER ONE

Paralyzing Darkness

The pain of life,
all too familiar,
God's loving hand,
beyond our reach.

I had just agreed to teach the young married Sunday school class when word came that Keith and Debbie had been in a car accident. They were out for a casual Sunday afternoon drive, and were approaching a quiet intersection in the suburbs. The light was green. As they entered the intersection, two teenage boys racing motorcycles approached from Keith's left. Seeing the light turn yellow and then red, one boy stopped. One did not.

The screaming motorcycle hit the rear door of their car at an estimated speed of 110 miles per hour, crushing it. The driver catapulted over the car and was killed instantly. Keith was in critical condition in the intensive care unit of a local hospital, but was expected to recover. Debbie was bruised, but otherwise physically unharmed. Rachel, their eleven-month-old daughter, their only child, was buckled securely in a protective child's car seat in the middle of the back seat . . . the safest possible place. She was almost untouched, the bruise on her left temple the only indication of the impact that broke her neck, killing her instantly.

When I got the news, I had never even met Keith and Debbie.

The weeks and months that followed were pure hell. Keith recovered physically and they returned to their active role with the Sunday school class. Keith, in his late twenties, was somewhat the "nutty professor," a young, studious systems engineer and an amateur evening futures trader. He thrust himself back into his profession and, at least outwardly, left the emotional tragedy behind.

Debbie, on the other hand, was alone, devastated, heartbroken, and paralyzed with questions . . . questions for which she had no answers. Virtually every Sunday for months, she would begin crying softly in the middle of our Sunday school class and quietly leave. Debbie was an attractive young woman in her early twenties, with beautiful features and an angelic innocence. She had been adopted as a child and experienced the love of a mother. That love, true motherly love, was deeply reflected in her pain. Her warmth, so naturally reflected in her kind smile, was missing. The brightness in her eyes had dimmed. Her very soul, a heart of pure kindness, was lost in emptiness, left with a world of reminders of her baby girl, and a husband disconnected from reality—his personal survival tactic. In all of her suffering, she only asked me one question. "Why?"

It wasn't a question that she asked to bring closure to a personal wound. It was asked out of total devastation and despair. It was asked through tears standing over an empty crib or holding one of Rachel's dresses that she no longer needed, but could not bear to let go of. Lost in darkness, searching for hope, she asked, "Why?" In the single, simple word "why," she was really asking, "Why . . . why in the midst of a living hell, can I not find understanding, guidance, peace . . . hope?"

Debbie looked to me for guidance, for help . . . for hope. I searched, stumbling, looking for words of encouragement and support, but I was of little help.

In that moment, for that season of life, Keith and Debbie were emotionally frozen in time, paralyzed, incapable of moving forward. But life, by its very nature, moves on. The sun rises and the sun sets. The world moves on at blinding speed, leaving those stunned and devastated in its path, losing ground, left behind.

Debbie would drift in emptiness, with a deep emotional void. She would search for comfort and peace. In total desperation, innocence, and blindness, she would pour her heart, soul, body, and mind into replacing Rachel, physically and emotionally. Keith continued alone on his path, just trying to move on. On autopilot, he walked into the office every day and punched the clock, in and out, in and out. He had always deeply desired to climb into the management ranks of his company, so he trudged forward with blinders on. Debbie and Keith were both numb to their surroundings. They were functioning mindlessly, like a military unit marching in step: left . . . left . . . left, right, left. Work . . . work . . . work, church, work.

Home, painfully empty, was peripheral to their world of survival. Even when they were home together, they were emotionally apart. I can still see Keith sitting in front of the computer analyzing the futures markets, the light from the monitor reflecting off of his glasses as he sat silently in the darkness of the guest bedroom.

Keith and Debbie were doing exactly what you or I would have done. They were grasping for something to hold onto, something they understood, and something that made sense. They were in uncharted waters, with no points of reference and no signs by which to navigate. Blind-sided by Rachel's unexpected death, they found their marriage relationship emotionally empty, and their spiritual foundation too weak to give them courage and hope.

They just moved on. So did I. My lack of spiritual insight and my inability to support Debbie and Keith caused me only temporary concern. It was not a major disruption in my life. Certainly time would be the great healer. They could have more children.

The tragic circumstances of life had dealt a painful blow, and we all just drifted mindlessly away, emotionally blinded and deeply wounded. In the paralyzing darkness, not one of us found even a glimmer of hope to begin healing the soul. We did not sense God's presence, hear His voice, nor feel His touch.

Each of us, in our own separate worlds, would face paralyzing darkness again—with no hope. We were all at great risk, and did not know it. Spiritual innocence can be very unkind.

CHAPTER TWO

Living in Innocence

I was born and reared in Macon, Georgia, in a conservative, middle-income family. The church was the cornerstone of our existence. I have extraordinary parents who represent the Bible Belt well. My dad served in World War II and the Korean War, moved to Macon in 1949, married my mother, and worked as a teacher and principal during his thirty-year career in public education. My mother worked for the Bibb County public school system as well, their work schedules creating unlimited family time in the afternoons and every summer. They provided a stable home environment, instilled high moral values, and were a living example.

Our dad effortlessly paved the way for my brother and me. He was active in church leadership, displayed open and honest love for our mother, and understood how you spell love to a child: T-I-M-E. My brother and I hunted, fished, golfed, and played sports—every sport. Dad coached and Mom kept the official scorebook. She taught me how. On Saturday afternoons I would watch the Yankees games on our black-and-white television set, keep the scorebook, and listen to Dizzy Dean's southern drawl. I was blessed with a healthy sense of self-confidence, and life seemed remarkably simple.

Every day of my youth, I lived and breathed in an atmosphere of honesty, trust, patience, and kindness—God in the flesh, the love of 1 Corinthians 13 alive in our home. I joyfully attended church every time they opened the doors, sang in the youth choir, and preached on Youth Sunday when I was sixteen. I made excellent grades, honored my parents, and displayed a heart of honesty and kindness.

With a solid foundation, my journey into adulthood began. Peacefully walking the straight and narrow path, I entered Georgia Tech as a freshman in the fall of 1974. Just like my brother, I married at age nineteen, following the completion of my first year in college. My bride, Jeannie, with high school diploma in hand, was a beautiful young woman—full of energy, with tenacity to tackle the world. She was eighteen years old.

I remember the day we met. On a sunny Saturday morning, in the summer of 1972, Jeannie and Delinda, a neighbor and common friend of ours, walked over to my house to tell me of the accidental drowning of a teenage friend. I was in the front yard trimming shrubs. Jeannie, just barely fifteen, had been to the beach with her family on vacation and had quite a suntan. Her heart-shaped face and her little pug nose showed just a hint of peeling. Her sleeveless shirt and modest shorts revealed both her physical beauty and her basic conservative nature. Her long brown hair was parted in the middle, neatly braided into two pigtails, both of which were pinned atop her head. She had a look of warmth and innocence about her. I thought she was incredibly cute.

Jeannie, her mom and dad, and her younger brother Mike lived just around the corner from us. Jeannie's spiritual upbringing mirrored mine. Reared in the church, she was quite the young Bible scholar, and she had embraced the great truths. We lived in the same middle-class neighborhood, sharing similar family and socioeconomic backgrounds. Our happenstance introduction would quickly evolve into a barrage of phone calls, frequent visits, and of course, the then-popular "going steady." Two years of steady dating led to a marriage proposal and a simple but beautiful engagement ring on Jeannie's finger. She was a rarity, a high-school senior engaged to be married.

One year later, our joyful teenage romance would lead us down the aisle. Our parents would watch in silence, supportive but anxious and understandably concerned. After the blur of "*I do*s" and an assembly line of well wishers, we drove away from the church with "Hot Springs Tonight" plastered on the rear window of our car. An excited friend of Jeannie's family yelled, "I didn't know they were going to Arkansas on their honeymoon!" Her naïveté mirrored ours.

As we left the church, it seemed remarkably like any other date, as if we were embarking on another trip to Six Flags Over Georgia with friends. As we pulled onto the main road, I looked in my rearview mirror at family and friends waving good-bye, patted Jeannie on her left leg, and kissed her.

The story of our wedding night is one of Jeannie's favorites, and she loves for me to tell it. It is both hilarious and, in retrospect, insightful. We stayed at a hotel on I-75 in South Georgia, en route to Florida. Having seen a billboard along the interstate that read "Kids 18 & Under Stay Free," I just simply could not resist it. I told the teenage boy at the check-in counter that my bride was eighteen years old, and I asked if she could stay free. Somewhat taken aback, he looked at me, looked down in apparent disbelief, thought for a moment, and then lifted his chin and said, "Sure." We had a great time on our honeymoon, leaving us with many fond memories. Jeannie and I were both remarkably happy, and equally clueless.

We moved to Atlanta, Georgia, the next week, and I entered my sophomore year of college. We "set up house," and I embraced the role of head of household with great ease. My brother, Jim, a graduating senior at Tech, and his wife, Theresa, moved out of the second-floor efficiency apartment in the married housing complex, and we moved in, right in step. I went to school full-time and worked part-time. Jeannie did just the opposite, she a part-time student and full-time employee at Georgia State University in downtown Atlanta—from yellow school buses to Marta, Atlanta's rapid transit system—in the blink of an eye.

We were counting our pennies, playing cards with our newfound church friends, playing putt-putt golf late at night when it was cheap, and generally having a blast. We both laugh with fond recollection of buying our first Christmas tree late one December night. As the owner was closing up shop, we searched and searched, and bought the top five-foot section cut out of a damaged ten-foot tree. We paid five dollars, and I got my first real taste of seeing Jeannie bargain hunt and negotiate. Decorating our own tree, our first tree together, was wonderful. Even as I write, my heart is reminded of our joyful two years in Atlanta.

I graduated from Georgia Tech on a Saturday morning, we moved to Durham, North Carolina, over Labor Day weekend, and I started classes at Duke University on Tuesday. We arrived in Durham with Jeannie expecting our first child. Staci, our oldest daughter, was born three months later during the week of my first semester final exams. Seventeen months later, with our son Dustin due any day, I walked off the stage, diploma in hand. As I entered my professional career, we moved to South Carolina and bought our first house. It was the perfect world—the American dream—just as we had imagined. We had our hands full with two children under the age of two, but Jeannie was a natural mom, and we managed with great ease.

Excellent professional opportunities came my way during the next ten years, and my upwardly mobile career took us from South Carolina, to Georgia, to Texas. We were truly blessed. I had the corner office at work, and our family continued to blossom. Every time Jeannie thought of completing her college degree, it seemed we were expecting another baby. We had three more beautiful girls, Amber, Dana, and Megan, along the journey from Georgia to Texas.

It did not take long to get properly introduced to Texas. Texans have a heart, a style, and a swagger all their own. We saw the bumper stickers, "I am from Texas, what country are you from?" That great truth would be displayed when we joined the church. The pastor stood before the large congregation and introduced us. I will never forget it. He smiled, placed his hand on my shoulder, and introduced me as the new administrator of the local hospital. He introduced Jeannie as my lovely wife and the mother of "all these beautiful children." He then went down the line . . . Staci, Dustin, Amber, Dana . . . and then he paused, and with great pride, he said, "and here is our Texan." We were welcome; we were "home-folk," because Megan, our infant daughter, was born in Texas. For all the humor in that story, it was true. Belonging, the sense of oneness, is a powerful concept. Texans understand it.

Our navy blue 1971 two-door Volvo had long since been retired and replaced with the then-popular brown and beige conversion van. We needed it. The kids loved the captain's chairs, the rear stereo system, and the back seat that reclined into a bed. The TV/VCR was indispensable on our nine-hundred-mile trip to visit family in Georgia. I have never seen the movie *The Little Mermaid*, but I heard the words and music over and over and over again as I drove into the night on I-20 between Texas and Georgia. With everyone securely buckled into their respective seats, we looked like the perfect family. With the children growing into adolescence, we were consumed with baseball, softball, gymnastics, cheerleading, dance, and piano—with Jeannie engulfed as the ultimate taxi mom. Friends marveled at her energy. Nobody was better.

As my professional path led us on our tour through the southeast and then westward to Texas, we were true to our spiritual roots, always very active in the church. Sunday morning took on a life of its own with an assembly line of hair curlers flying, matching outfits, slips, pantyhose, and hair bows, with our son intent on steering clear of the bedlam. It was an awesome sight and quite a memory. We attended church every Sunday with Bibles in hand, participated in virtually every church-related activity, and prayed at every meal. We looked the part. One by one, our children were coming to know the Lord personally and we rejoiced. We were the envy of family and friends. A friend laughed and called us "Ken and Barbie." From all appearances, we were.

Appearances can be deceiving. For all of the joy and happiness in our family, Jeannie and I had one major struggle, and it was a very troubling, unresolved problem. Early in our marriage, we had extreme difficulty solving our personal conflicts. We had never overcome it.

Now, with the pace of life at breakneck speed, it was all we could do to stay afloat. We had very little time to dedicate to each other. We were almost always in the same room, but rarely ever together, really together.

Our backgrounds, as remarkably similar as they were, had one very unique difference. I had grown up in a home blanketed with peace and tranquility. Never, not once, in my entire life had I heard either of my parents raise their voices to each other, to my brother, or to me . . . *never*. Every disciplinary measure, every discussion, took place at the round kitchen table, bathed in calmness. Each round-table discussion, with my dad's steady hand in charge, ended in understanding, politeness, and general agreement. I had never experienced anything else. I am not suggesting that such an environment is altogether good. In fact, it is not. But it was all that I knew.

Jeannie, on the other hand, grew up in a dynamic environment that I like to call "the door slammers"—figuratively speaking. Her family spoke their minds, directly and aggressively. Everyone knew where everyone else stood. If a grenade was thrown in the room, it was uneventful. In fact, it was quite effective. No hidden agendas, no surprises.

Both approaches are effective. They work equally well until you put two naïve teenagers together in a marriage in an efficiency apartment and leave them alone to figure it out. We didn't.

One simple story set the stage for our lives. One Saturday morning in the peace and quietness of our apartment at Georgia Tech, I was sitting on the sofa reading the newspaper. Jeannie, very frustrated about something that neither of us now remembers, sat down beside me and began to speak her mind. With the initial hint of tightness in my chest, I held my paper steady and casually glanced in her direction. In the absence of my undivided attention, she spoke up louder and asked, "Are you going to listen to me?" I politely folded the newspaper in my lap and stared directly into her eyes as she unloaded. Her momentary tirade was explosive. She then stopped abruptly and said, "That's all I have to say." Being in uncharted waters and not knowing what else to do, I calmly opened my newspaper and continued to read. I did not know what the right answer was, but in the next instant, I knew what the wrong answer was. I got my first real introduction to the meaning of the "door-slammer," up close and in person.

A few moments later she was over it, acting as if nothing ever happened. I thought my chest was going to explode. We solved little or nothing that Saturday morning, and our inability to confront and resolve our differences would haunt us for years and years to come. Jeannie blew her stack, I shut down, and that became our standard solution. The appearance of perfection was a myth.

"Ken and Barbie" we were not. The dynamics of the Saturday morning newspaper story would play out again and again in our lives, and the impact of our inability to resolve our problems would mount. Our external challenges in life seemed insignificant, but our internal pressure cooker, though unseen, was a constant nagging problem for both of us. Frustrating conversations would occasionally deteriorate into Jeannie saying, "I don't think you love me. I don't think you have ever loved me." Reading the cue cards of the straight and narrow path, I would respond, "Of course I love you. How could you say that?" Staring into the darkness of the moment, we would both move on to the next baseball game, our polished external image of perfection shining brightly.

Despite the growing struggle behind the scenes in our marriage, we were ahead of the curve in life, successful on all fronts. The phone rang, and the career opportunity of a lifetime came my way. In the words of one of Willie Nelson's most popular songs, we were "On the Road Again." We packed up the kids and headed east to Nashville, Tennessee. The simplicity of life and my sense of personal accomplishment filled me with great pride . . . more success, more blindness, more risk.

Our well-intentioned journey through life was invisibly off course. Our false image of "Ken and Barbie with kids" had camouflaged a deep-seated problem. God was present and accounted for, but He was not alive in our hearts. He did not have a seat at the table when it came decision-making time. We had relegated God to a passive observer, neatly "in His place" in our lives. Nobody knew, not even us. Innocence and naïveté, both personal and spiritual, would create tremendous risk and open the doors for a journey deep in sin. The devastating pain would be shared by the guilty and innocent alike. The storm clouds gathering on the horizon would approach unnoticed, as if in the darkness of the night. How could the impossible happen?

This true story, a simple story of my mother's childhood, provides great insight, a crystal clear picture . . . of the impossible: My mother, a kind, mild-mannered woman with a heart for others, grew up in south Georgia, the only surviving child of a sharecropping family. Her two siblings died in their infancy, the result of poor medical information and attention. As a young teenager, she came home from school early in the spring to help her father farm and to walk behind a mule, plowing. She, like her friends, grew up in a house with no insulation, no indoor plumbing, and no electricity.

Her family rose before daybreak, worked hard to put food on the table, and went to bed "with the chickens." On occasion they would venture down the dirt road on Saturday, to the house of the only friend who had an AM radio, and listen to the *Grand Ole Opry* "crackling" in the night. That was her life. From time to time over the years, she would share stories from the "good ole days."

As a curious teenager, one day I asked her what it was like for her to be poor, really poor. I have vivid recollection of the moment. She smiled and told me, "*I did not know that I was poor.*" Everybody she knew sharecropped. They were all poor. Every family's Christmas tree was a pine cut from the woods. All of her friends were lucky if they got one present. They just scraped by. She was just like everybody else.

My spiritual journey into adulthood mirrored my mother's childhood upbringing. I was "poor" in my understanding of the living presence of God, and I did not know it. I was an active participant in church, and I had a strong intellectual sense of who God was. My spiritual understanding was deeply ingrained. I carried my Bible with comfort, but I did not read God's Word with any regularity. I did not grasp God at a personal level. I envisioned the Lord of the Universe sitting on a distant throne overlooking His subjects, passing judgment. Many of the hellfire and brimstone sermons of my youth both encouraged and supported my belief. My spiritual development, immature as it was, seemed right to me. My involvement in church activities and participation in positions of leadership were remarkably normal. I taught Sunday school and was asked to be a deacon. I fit right in, and I looked just like almost everybody else. I was sharecropping, living in spiritual poverty, and did not know it.

This is one of the greatest risks that we, the people of God, face in the modern-day church. We have settled in comfortably and we are spiritually content.

Sadly, our Christianity, our personal walk with God,
is defined primarily by
our relationships with Christian friends
and our involvement in church activities.
The person of God is nowhere to be found.

God is absent. We attend church regularly, follow along in our Bibles attentively as the pastor preaches or our Sunday school teacher facilitates, listen intently to prayer requests and make written notes, read current invigorating spiritual literature, tithe, participate in positions of church leadership, and make certain our children participate in all church-related activities. We prepare and send food when there is a need in the church family, send appropriate cards, and joyfully attend church-related social functions. To the outside world, we look and sound remarkably "Christian," especially on Sundays.

Like clay in the hands of the potter,
we mold our image, our exterior, our spiritual shell,
to reflect the image of Christ.

It is not a game. We are not pretending. We are sincerely, honorably seeking to do the right thing. But spiritual share-cropping, the "way that seems right to a man," without God as our spiritual Father and guide, "in the end . . . leads to [spiritual] death" (Prov. 16:25).

The evolution of our spiritual journey is somewhat fascinating. The church has become the epicenter of our spiritual existence. The fact that the church itself has gained a position of such dominance in our spiritual walk is both remarkable and dangerous. It is not the message Jesus conveyed in His teachings. In fact, Jesus spoke only once of the church itself. It was not His focus. His guidance steered His followers away from a world of regulations and focused on a personal relationship. He was constantly battling with the Pharisees who existed in a world of structure and rules. In the fifteenth chapter of Matthew, echoing God's words to the prophet Isaiah, Jesus said:

> These people honor me with their lips,
> but their hearts are far from me.
> They worship me in vain;
> their teachings are but rules taught by men (vv. 8–9).

Jesus came to turn us away from those binding restrictions, free us, and save us from the law. Given His consistent, clear teaching and guidance, we should pause and ponder how we have come to this place. . . . It is remarkably simple.

A brief trip into the world of little-league baseball is telling. First, a dad and his child are playing catch in the front yard of their home. It is not long before several neighborhood children join in, the kids choose teams, and the game begins. Local rules apply. The small oak tree is the left-field foul pole, the worn spot by the basketball goal is second base, and a ball hit over the neighbors' chain link fence is both a homerun and an out. Day after day, the children gather to play, until they yearn for competition. They gather at the local park to play a group of children from a nearby subdivision.

The parents hear of the games and see this as a real opportunity to develop the talent of their youngsters. A league is formed. The parents gather and establish bylaws, vote for league officers, and agree on rules. Not long afterwards, coaches have back-room meetings to manipulate the system to get the best players and aggressively prepare for the opening day of the season. Coaches stand toe-to-toe with the umpires arguing balls and strikes, and moms and dads are hanging on the fence living vicariously through their innocent children—who just wanted to play catch in the front yard with their parents.

All of our children played organized sports, and I am a big supporter. I value the principles of team play and competition that they teach. The preceding analysis of little-league baseball, while often true, really has nothing to do with baseball at all. There is a powerful spiritual message embedded in our modern-day little-league story. It is about our spiritual journey through life. We pull off the little-league World Series with pomp and circumstance, and we have a structured practice schedule for the team, but we have come to a place that almost no children are standing in the front yard playing catch. We conduct the impressive and extraordinarily important Sunday service with bulletproof precision, and conduct class after class; yet we as individuals lack the desire and discipline to read God's Word and spend heartfelt time in our prayer life. We have forgotten who brought us to the dance . . . or perhaps we never knew.

God Himself has spoken directly to this subject. In the first chapter of Isaiah, God simply said, they do "not know, my people do not understand" (v. 3). As His chosen people veered off course, they turned their backs on the very person of God. Yet, they continued their public worship. Their exterior spiritual image was fully intact.

They were consistent, very "religious," in their legalistic world of offerings, assemblies, and feasts. Despite their public display, God Himself said, "They have become a burden to me; I am weary of bearing them" (v. 14). God was basically tired of their lack of personal commitment, and He told Isaiah the prophet how frustrated He was. God displayed deep emotions, sincere feelings, as He told Isaiah, ". . . my soul hates" (v. 14) their game. The words from God's own heart reveal His disgust for their failure to understand and His hatred for a false spiritual image. Hate is a very strong word when spoken from the heart of the living God. We should take notice.

Patrick Morley, in his book *Second Wind for the Second Half*, speaks to the heart of this subject:

> Our culture has a small view of God. A small view of God has led to a small response, even among people of faith. We are producing a generation of Christians who are orthodox in belief but secular in behavior. In other words, they have the "right belief" but not the "right practice." The Bible calls this disobedience.

It is truly frightening. The church, the body of believers, has evolved to a place of personal spiritual poverty, "right belief" without "right practice," without ever realizing it. The church has lost its spiritual compass and heart. Our personal relationship with the living God, the Lord Himself, is limited, often non-existent. David's words in Psalm 143, meant for every one of us, are too often an unfamiliar language:

> . . . I meditate on all your works
> and consider what your hands have done.

I spread out my hands to you;

my soul thirsts for you like a parched land. . . .

Let the morning bring me word of your unfailing love,

for I have put my trust in you.

Show me the way I should go,

for to you I lift up my soul (v. 5–6, 8).

Meditating on God's Word, thirsting for the presence of God, trusting, and lifting up our souls to Him tend to be unfamiliar concepts to us. Struggling to get to church on time and rushing to get out of the parking lot to beat the lunch crowd is more our style. Our spiritual naïveté leaves us unfamiliar with, and disconnected from, the person of God.

> *Therefore,* unawareness,
> *not disobedience,*
> *is often the driving force in our failure*
> *to have a meaningful*
> *personal relationship with the Lord.*

We play in the big game and we practice with the team, but we do not take the time to practice throwing, catching, and batting . . . the basics. We simply do not grasp that "The Lord Almighty is with us" (Ps. 46:7). We have come to view Moses and the burning bush as a cute children's Bible story, and we fail to see that it is the vivid image of the living God seeing the misery, hearing the cries, expressing His heartfelt concern, and showing commitment to rescue His people (Exod. 3:7–8). In our everyday lives, we have excluded the person of God.

We have modified God's plan to fit our personal agendas. We have taken the book of Job and manipulated it to be a book about "great patience," a comfort zone for us. It is, in fact, a replica of how we often live, and who I had become. In the twenty-ninth chapter, Job proudly says:

> I was eyes to the blind
> and feet to the lame.
> I was father to the needy;
> I took up the case of the stranger.
> Men listened to me . . .
> I chose the way for them . . .
> I dwelt as a king . . .
> I was like one who comforts . . . (vv. 15–16, 21, 25).

Job was living a life of "I, I, I, me, me, me," with God as an onlooker. Job was the provider, taking care of everything, with God effectively uninvolved. In the end, after years of painful suffering, Job surrendered. Job, a man who had a reputation of fearing God and shunning evil (Job 1:1), had been honestly wrong in his understanding of who God was. He confessed to the Lord, saying, "My ears had heard of you but now my eyes have seen you" (Job 42:5).

We, like Job, need to grow to see God as
"Who we serve," not just "Why we serve."

We need to put that "Saturday morning newspaper" down and open our eyes to the truth. It is time to look in the mirror and be honest with ourselves about who we are and how God fits into our lives. As Jim Collins writes in the book *Good to Great,* we need to "confront the brutal facts."

I had heard, but I had not seen. The truth was not on my radar screen. I was pretending. Thus, in my innocent, spiritually camouflaged world of pride, "I, I, I . . . me, me, me," the unthinkable could, and would, happen. My personal path of blindness and sinfulness would lead our family astray into a world of darkness. God, wanting to rescue me, would watch and suffer, as "I" went alone.

CHAPTER THREE

The Lone Ranger

"'Though you soar like the eagle
and make your nest among the stars,
from there I will bring you down,'
declares the Lord."
—Obadiah 1:4

We arrived in Nashville, and I was riding the crest of the professional wave. Corporate America, with all its notoriety and possibilities, was in my grasp. At age thirty-eight, I was a professional rocket ship, younger than all of my peers and most of my subordinates. When I traveled across the country, my title demanded respect, and my personal responsibility for hundreds of millions of dollars in company revenue buoyed my ego. I was on cruise control. With a solid foundation, good skills, a good education, and a bit of good fortune along the way, I had arrived. I quickly learned the real meaning of bonuses and stock options. It could only get better. Unfortunately, God's modern-day messages in Proverbs were not on my radar screen.

Pride goes before destruction, a haughty spirit before a fall (16:18).

When pride comes, then comes disgrace, but with humility comes
wisdom (11:2).

Pride, the very fullness of self and absence of God, would have
a blinding effect on me. Destruction and disgrace would engulf my
life. As I mentioned in the prior chapter, I carried my Bible with
great comfort and ease, but I knew very little about it. It is impossible to embrace the heart of God, to trust God and thirst for Him,
when you do not read and know His Word. This is a critical
concept, and I will give it further attention in chapter nine.

It is one thing to be spiritually naïve, unaware of the living presence of God. It is an entirely different matter to be self-centered and
prideful. Make no mistake; I knew the difference between right and
wrong. I was not a Bible scholar, but I knew the Bible specifically
addressed the sinfulness of man. My deep heritage in the church
made it impossible to miss the Ten Commandments, and I knew
adultery was there. I would not be surprised by that fact.

Given my deep spiritual roots, even if I did not have a regular
working relationship with the Lord, how could I possibly drift from
my committed roles of husband, father, respected health-care professional, and Sunday school teacher, to the dark world of infidelity? The
impossible, the unbelievable would happen with shocking ease. My
lone-ranger lifestyle, a journey of independence from God and family,
created constant exposure and personal risk. The lack of a consistent
accountability to my Maker and to my wife would make way for a
trickle of water in a distant mountain stream to grow quietly, unde-
tected, into a raging flood.

The fact that my family and friends did not see it coming is not
really surprising. My carefully orchestrated secret life kept them in

darkness. However, it would seem unlikely that I, rafting the waters daily, could drift blindly. Do not be mistaken.

My downhill slide did not begin with the presence of sin, but with the absence of God as my guide.

It began when we said, "I do," in 1975, and naïvely relegated our Maker to a God that we reached out to only in times of trouble. Ingrained, unaddressed sin is not the problem; it is the symptom of an absentee Savior.

The absence of God, the very presence of pride and self-centeredness in our daily walk, exposes us to tremendous danger, a concept that I will call *invisible risk*. The following analogy about the process of aging conveys this great truth of *invisible risk*: not one of us has ever looked into the mirror on two consecutive days and said, "I look older than I did yesterday." Yet, a quick glance at a picture from ten years ago reveals the undeniable truth. We are getting older. We look older every day, but the change is so minute, so insignificant, that it is undetectable, invisible. We are constantly changing, every day, for better or for worse, most often unnoticed. There are no warning sirens, no alarms. There is no yellow flashing light on the dashboard of life alerting us to "Low Fuel." So are our lives.

In the chapter about spiritual innocence, we discussed the tremendous risk of misunderstanding who God is . . . of knowing about Him, but not seeing Him. *Invisible risk*, the prideful path of the lone ranger, is equally dangerous. God's absence makes way for the ego to blossom, and allows us to drift one heartbeat at a time, invisibly, unnoticed— one smile, one wink, one touch of the hand, and one casual luncheon date, never intending to veer off course, never seeing it.

Many of you, light-years away from my nightmare of adultery, will be inclined to dismiss this concept of *invisible risk*. You will conclude that it is simply not applicable in your life, and you will move on. Let me extend a word of caution:

> *If you do not believe that the concept of invisible risk*
> *is a danger zone for you,*
> *then you are **the** person at the greatest possible risk.*

I have shared this statement many times. Again and again, I have seen frowns and looks of disbelief on the faces of adult men and women. Years ago, a woman in our young married Sunday school class heard me teach this very principle. Three months later, she sat in my office at lunchtime one day, weeping uncontrollably, lost in an affair that literally took her by storm. She told me, "I heard what you said, but I never believed it could happen to me. I didn't really even listen."

Honestly, if you see no personal risk, you will turn your head, blind and unaware, and fail to see the early warning signs. The eroding, crippling effect of the sinful nature will undermine you, second by second, minute by minute, hour by hour, day by day, and it will go unnoticed.

> *Invisible risk is not about adultery.*
> *It is about our basic sinful nature*
> *that sends us adrift, off course, losing focus,*
> *one heartbeat at a time.*

Our society is quick to identify flagrantly sinful behaviors, and to pass judgment. Transgressions such as sexual immorality, impurity, and drunkenness are addressed biblically, are highly visible, and garner a lot of attention. Our tendency is to stand around, point fingers, and be thankful that we are not involved. We tend to be far less mindful of sinful "attitudes" such as hatred, jealousy, selfish ambition, and dissensions that can just as easily undermine us. The fifth chapter of Galatians gives them equal attention. Paul follows with a discussion of the fruit of the Spirit, addressing love, joy, peace, patience, and self-control.

We are all constantly sowing seeds in life, either spiritual or sinful, and it happens invisibly. Though unnoticed, we are constantly either growing into God's presence or drifting away from Him. Such is the nature and certainty of *invisible risk*.

At this very moment, even as you read, you are sowing seeds. Your relationship with the Lord and, if you are married, with your spouse, is changing every day. It is either better or worse than it was yesterday or last week, but the difference is minimal, insignificant, and invisible. I would encourage you to stop, take a mental image of your current relationship with your spouse, your children, and the Lord, and compare that image with where you stood one year ago, three years ago, and five years ago. For better or for worse, the relationships are different, and you will see it. You will know it.

If you have lost ground, grasp this moment, and take the opportunity to confront the truth, reverse your deteriorating course, and make a commitment to recover, one day at a time. Redirecting our path is a marathon, not a one-hundred-yard dash, and it takes time and energy. I will give this topic further attention in chapter nine.

Solomon speaks wisely and gives counsel in the book of Proverbs. "The prudent see danger and take refuge, but the simple keep going and suffer for it" (27:12). Note our journey of independence in Solomon's words. God gives us the freedom to go it alone. It is our choice. Our decision to exclude God is a blank check for the sinful nature to "keep going and suffer," to erode our lives. *Invisible risk*, the enemy, the very essence of the sinful nature, "masquerades as an angel of light." *Invisible risk* lurks in the shadows and, not surprisingly, parades as a servant of righteousness (2 Cor. 11:14). This is an undeniable truth.

The journey of the personal will, with the living God watching from a distance, is a long, lonely road. My walk alone, with God nicely seated as a welcomed spectator in my life, collapsed. Paul reminds us, "A man reaps what he sows. The one who sows to please his sinful nature . . . will reap destruction" (Gal. 6:7–8). My youthful spiritual innocence had evolved into an adulthood of blinding sin and disobedience. The storm hit and it was furious.

Out of honor, respect, and deep love for my wife and our children, I will not share unnecessary graphic details. But I will say this:

The path of blinding adultery,
the harsh reality of unbridled sin,
is a horrific experience that shatters lives, destroys trust,
and leads you to question God's very existence.

The memories of devastated teenage daughters screaming at me in pain and disbelief, a youthful teenage son thrust instantly into the impossible roles of referee and peacemaker, streams of tears flooding innocent faces, and nights of shell-shocked silence are forever imprinted on my soul. I have vivid recollection of the picture of their broken hearts painted tearfully on their faces. They really just wanted to know one thing—they wanted to know why their daddy did not love them anymore. At those horrific moments, I could not open my mouth. I could not speak. There was no need to. My actions had already spoken to them . . . very loudly.

My journey into darkness impacted every member of our family, no one more painfully than my wife. Jeannie was forced to be in my physical presence due to our many family obligations, but the distant, haunting look in her eyes revealed fear and separation. When in the same room, she would step aside, careful to avoid my touch as I passed by. She would physically and emotionally recoil if our hands accidentally brushed together. The bubbly teenager, the wife of my youth, was missing in action. She had become a prisoner of war. Jeannie, in her physical being, moved about the house and amongst the children carrying out her obligatory duties, but her heart was nowhere to be found.

The younger girls kept their distance and watched in silence. They were unsure of exactly what was happening. They were less certain of what tomorrow would bring. They had friends whose parents had divorced, and they had seen their pain, witnessed their tears, and shared their struggles. They assumed they were next in line, and unlike softball and cheerleading, they did not know how to practice or prepare for divorce. The fear in their faces needed no words of explanation.

The emotional scars were deep. The damage was extensive, impossible to quantify, but I knew it was severe. I could feel it. I could see it. I could hear it. Innocence, precious innocence, was gone. Jeannie and the children, once eager to give their hearts to me, now kept their emotional distance, watching carefully. My words, the words they had once embraced as truth, had turned out to be littered with lies.

My spontaneous smile and the natural sparkle in my eyes were gone. They had been replaced with a lifeless stone-faced stare . . . looking, but rarely seeing. My mother always said that she could read my emotions by the look on my face. Now, I could simply walk into a room and everybody knew—I was losing control, losing my grip on life.

In the darkest hours, in the valley of the shadow of death, I told our family counselor, "If I knew where God kept the time clock to life, I would clock out." I had always heard of the men who went to the corner grocery store late at night to buy bread and milk, and then simply disappeared into thin air, leaving their wives and children behind to fend for themselves. Twenty years later they would show up on a television show, living under an assumed name in some small town in Montana. I was always curious. What set of circumstances could possibly motivate any human being to simply walk away from his or her commitments and obligations? Now I knew. If not for the overwhelming sense of family obligations instilled by my dad, I think I would have simply "clocked out," and walked away.

My sky-rocketing career stalled. Bonuses and stock options with retirement written all over them disappeared. I moved on. Nothing really seemed to matter anymore. The primary agenda in life was now survival, and that seemed highly unlikely.

I was unprepared and ill-equipped. Like a prizefight, it was round one, round two, round three, round four, round five . . . with blood streaming down my face almost every time I returned to my corner. One minute to rest, and the bell would ring for the next round. I would win an occasional round, but I was growing closer and closer to certain defeat. It appeared highly unlikely the fight would go the distance. A knockout seemed inevitable.

From time to time I wondered what God would do next, the great chess player on high observing my failures and moving the pawns of life. This analogy is not meant to be creative or playful. It is exactly what I thought, what I believed. No matter what I had ever said or taught in Sunday school, that is who I thought God really was, and I was a pawn. I was waiting and watching for God's next move. I was in survival mode.

The simplicity and joy of life, baseball and cheerleading, hair curlers and matching outfits, seemed but a distant memory, never to be recovered. They had been replaced with broken hearts and a world of uncertainty so evident in Dana, our ten-year-old daughter, left to cry alone on the floor of her daddy's empty closet.

Years later, Dana would write the following poem for a friend. The words echo like the silent voice of a little girl, sitting on the floor, lost in emotional darkness. Read them carefully. They are shockingly accurate, a vivid description of devastating pain. You may find these powerful words all too familiar. You may be living them. I was. We all were.

Overload

Overloaded, hung on life
My emotions turn against me, and stab me like a knife,

I'm looking ahead, but I don't see,
My thoughts are dominating me,

It used to be easy, to fake happiness and lie,
But I can't hide it when I cry,

You think you know everything,
But you should try seeing what I've been seeing,

This life's not as easy as I thought
I question if this battle is worth being fought,

My mind feels like it's going to explode,
But I can't help it, my emotions are in overload.

I had faked it, pretended as long as I could. I seriously questioned if the battle was worth being fought. I thought my mind would explode. I was on a steady diet of Tylenol and family counseling—survival tactics. At the time, neither seemed very helpful.

My family and my life were crumbling around me. I drifted mindlessly, struggling to piece together what looked like total destruction. In my darkest hour, I just tried to remember to breathe. I had *always* had the answers, and now I had none. For twenty years, my entire adult life, I had lived in total dependence on myself, successfully navigating the personal and professional challenges of life. I had come to what tragically seemed like the end. I was alone. I had never been alone before.

Years earlier, when Debbie, childless and alone, had wept in search of an answer, I did not have one. Eight years later, I still didn't. This time, it was *our* "major disruption," so I couldn't just "move on" as I had done then. Now, personally responsible for much of our pain, and accountable to God, Jeannie, and our children, life had melted through my fingers. I, like Debbie, felt emptiness.

When she and Keith had faced uncharted waters with no directional buoys, they had embraced the past, what they knew, motherhood and work, and trudged forward . . . without hope. I did the same. I searched deep within my heart and soul, gathered all that I had left, and forged ahead, committed to do the "right" thing, relying on willpower and determination. I had no other choice. Go it alone . . . it was all I knew.

I wallowed in darkness, going through the motions, for months. I was distracted at my new job, a zombie at church, lifeless in my marriage, and emotionally disconnected from our children. But I continued to march with the family—left . . . left . . . left, right, left. Work . . . work . . . work, church, work. I attended church religiously, but I was not particularly interested in God's input. I assumed that He probably was not paying attention, and if by chance He was, I very seriously doubted He had the right answer.

Dustin, our son who is spiritual beyond his years, extended his hand and tried to lift me up. He could not reach me. I was the lone ranger, a mere spiritual shell of a man; out of touch and out of reach.

The tragedy continued for another three years. I directed my path. Though not connected personally to God, I was knowledgeable of the truth. I knew what was right, but I could not grasp it. I did not understand the presence of God. The pain continued, the gift of His grace well beyond my reach.

Our lives had settled down to a general state of just existing. With a strong personal commitment to the cause, we had survived, but that was the extent of it. The imagery of "Ken and Barbie" had gone down in flames, but the children were safe and on their journeys. Perhaps that was all there was, and maybe that was enough.

Our two oldest children, Staci and Dustin, had finished college and were well on their way to beginning their own families. Amber was doing well in college, and Dana and Megan were in those challenging teen years. We were entering the final stretch, and though the words were never spoken, I think Jeannie and I were both just hanging on, trying to get our damaged plane on the ground. We were on final approach, with landing gear down. Our tanks were empty. We were gliding, simply hopeful of getting the wheels on the runway.

Debbie and Keith had preceded us down this path of desperation, and they had come up just short of the runway. They had turned to what they knew, their respective comfort zones, the pursuit of motherhood and a professional career, and they forged straight ahead. It had been their only source of hope.

Rachel's tragic death—an event of such pure innocence—and my sinful journey into the depths of despair, while shockingly different circumstances, had one pure thread of commonality. Both horrifically painful events in life required hope to heal the heart and soul, and each of us who were involved charted a course for survival that depended exclusively on personal willpower and determination. God's absence from our souls resulted in a downward spiral of the heart, an emotional tragedy.

Our individual responses, while tragic, can only be characterized as normal. Whether it is through simple non-belief, spiritual unawareness, or an independent lone-ranger lifestyle, we have relegated the living God to the role of observer, a position of weakness in our lives. We have embraced circumstances, the ups and downs of life, as the driving force in our daily decision-making. The result is most often a downward emotional spiral . . . cyclical misery. Sadly, it is our basic human nature.

In the following chapter, I will pause from our personal journey and expand on the concept of basic human nature. It is extraordinarily important that we grasp this great truth, for it is the quicksand of life which paralyzes, suffocates, and destroys. It is the great struggle that "hinders" and "so easily entangles" us (Heb. 12:1).

Chapter four, "Human Nature," will give insight and understanding into our everyday thinking, our decision-making process, and the spiritual pitfalls we face when the living God is relegated to the role of part-time participant in our lives. Joyfully, we will find the first glimmer of hope, the presence of the living God, His strength . . . revealed in our weakness.

Human Nature

"This is what the Lord says:
'Cursed is the one who trusts in man,
who depends on flesh for his strength
and whose heart turns away from the Lord.
He will be like a bush in the wastelands;
he will not see prosperity when it comes.
He will dwell in the parched places of the desert,
in a salt land where no one lives.'"
—Jeremiah 17:5–6

In chapter three, the journey of the lone ranger vividly and painfully illustrated the emotional tragedies that occur when we encounter difficult circumstances and depend on our personal willpower and determination for survival. This is our struggle.

Once again, we have great insight and guidance as God Himself speaks directly to this very issue in the thirty-first chapter of Isaiah. In the midst of great personal difficulty, the Lord cautions the Israelites against seeking the support of the Egyptians, who rely on horses, a multitude of chariots, and the "great strength" of their horsemen. Simply stated, the Egyptians depended exclusively on "the flesh"—humankind's resources, willpower, and determination.

We must take note. God is standing in the street and waving red flags of danger, trying to protect His people. He warns them. He warns us. The Egyptians did not "seek help from the Lord." They relegated God to the role of observer. They relied on the flesh, not the spirit. This is the very essence of our daily battle . . . the flesh versus the spirit. Teams have been chosen and the game is on. In our dependence on our willpower and determination, it is our natural tendency to embrace "the flesh"—the wrong team.

This chapter, the presentation of the Human Cycle, visually displays our basic decision-making style, our human nature, and the tragic impact on us when the circumstances of life (the flesh) dictate our everyday thought processes and we relegate our relationship with God (the spirit) to a secondary role.

Figure 1, the basic format of the Human Cycle, displays "circumstances" and our "relationship with God" as the two primary factors that impact our thinking in the decision-making process. For ease of explanation, circumstances are defined as being either "good" or "bad"; and our relationship with the Lord as either "weak" or "strong." I am acutely aware that there are degrees of each, in fact both are a continuum, but this simplistic approach will effectively serve our purpose of communicating the concept of the Human Cycle without diluting the message. As we reflect upon the twenty-ninth chapter of Job as discussed in chapter three, we should not overlook the fact that a weak relationship with God in this diagram is consistent with, in fact identical to, an extra dose of self, of "I, I, I, me, me, me." Simply stated, it is less of God, more of self, a concept that we are all too familiar with.

For presentation purposes, I have chosen "bad circumstances in life and a weak relationship with God" as our starting point (see fig. 1). In the midst of my personal journey, this was precisely my condition. My life had effectively collapsed and I had placed God at arm's

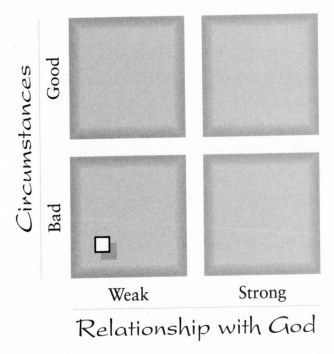

Fig. 1.

length, the ultimate football stiff-arm. To say this might be both an understatement and somewhat misleading. Exactly where was God and why? These questions are important, the answers powerful.

There is a very significant hidden point here, another golden nugget for the soul. I do not want you to miss it. All difficult circumstances in life provide a tremendous opportunity for personal spiritual growth. It is Paul's message to us. When I am weak, God steps up and I find strength in Him.

In the course of my journey, I had come to the place of harboring ingrained, unaddressed sinful behavior. I embraced it. This sinful existence was not limited to my actions. It reached beyond what I was doing and began to reflect who I was. It engulfed both my conduct and my character.

God does not, will not, and cannot rest quietly in the innermost part of the human heart and soul when the sinful nature is being harbored. It is impossible. If sin resides on the inside, God is on the outside. Thus, with the very essence of the sinful nature embodied in my character, God could not be present. God could not rest inside my circle. He departed. I placed Him at a distance—outside my circle, outside the boundaries of my soul, unable to be heard. I was in a soundproof booth, with God on the outside.

Herein lies the simple, yet spiritually powerful hidden truth:

We cannot embrace and harbor unaddressed, ingrained sinful behaviors or attitudes and simultaneously experience the living presence of our loving God.

We want to. We try to. So often we dabble in the realm of the sinful nature and attempt to keep God on a string. We fall victim to embracing the very essence of sin, and seek to camouflage our innermost thoughts. We walk the path of unbridled sin and polish our exterior Christ-like image. We try to juggle both balls. We cannot. We fail. It is impossible. We cannot embrace, care for, and love the sinful nature and also walk with God. Nor can we walk in God's path and harbor a sinful behavior or attitude. The very moment we engage with God, we chart a new course, and we desire in our heart to oust the sinful nature from our soul. The Bible simply and directly says that no man or woman can simultaneously embrace both. We will be devoted to the sinful nature and stiff-arm God, or vice versa. You cannot serve two masters (Luke 16:13).

There is nothing overly insightful or magical about this great spiritual truth. Yet, I dedicate attention to it because it is such a huge pitfall for us. Again and again, we try the impossible. We search for a way to keep both fires burning, only to blindly, in the secret of the darkness, embrace the sinful nature and "fake it" spiritually. We polish God up, put Him outside our inner circle, and relegate Him to the hidden role of observer. That is exactly what I did. It is remarkably clear to me now. Yet, in the midst of the sinful journey, the gray zone of the world seemed massive. The presence of ingrained sin has an amazing ability to neutralize the heart's and mind's awareness and attention to right and wrong. I learned this truth in the school of hard knocks.

With God relegated to the role of onlooker, I searched deep within my soul and struggled forward, committed to do my best to solve our problems. This is our normal, standard response to life's dilemmas . . . go it alone, leaving God outside the circle in a weak position, observing. Consistent with my thought processes, we question whether or not God is listening at all, and highly doubt He has the right answer anyway. So why bother asking Him?

As reflected in figure 2, we go it alone, often realizing moderate success, a reprieve from our horrendous circumstances. That temporary success is, in and of itself, dangerous because it boosts our confidence in self to overcome adversity. Richard Foster, in the introductory chapter of *Celebration of Discipline*, addresses this point powerfully. He provides in-depth spiritual insight into the concept of "will worship, the stifling slavery of self-interest." I highly recommend reading it. The following excerpt is relevant to our journey together:

Willpower will never succeed in dealing with the deeply ingrained habits of sin. Emmet Fox writes, "As soon as you resist mentally any undesirable or unwanted circumstance, you thereby endow it with more power—power which it will use against you, and you will have depleted your own resources to that exact extent." Heini Arnold concludes, "As long as we think we can save ourselves by our own willpower, we will only make the evil in us stronger than ever." "Will worship" may produce an outward show of success for a time, but in the cracks and crevices of our lives, our deep inner condition will eventually be revealed. People can make a good showing for a time, but sooner or later there will come that unguarded moment when the "careless word" will slip out to reveal the true condition of the heart.

This was certainly true for me. My new job opportunity gave me a sense of professional stability, and our marital separation was

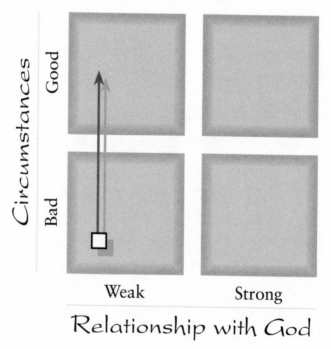

Fig. 2.

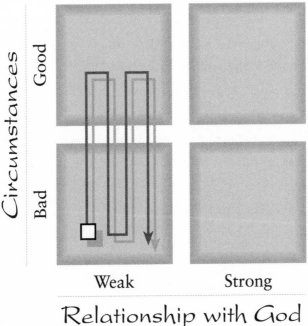

Fig. 3.

short-lived. Despite the seriousness of our problems, I still "had it."
I had not lost my touch. I landed on my feet again, the cat with nine
lives. "I" had effectively solved my problem, and I moved forward.
In the process, I had done little or nothing to alter my sinful direction
in life or my relationship with the Lord. Not surprisingly, the
improvement in our circumstances would be brief . . . more of the
same, with God at a distance.

Figure 3 represents a repeat of this cycle of "self," our normal
response. It is predictable, and it is progressively dangerous. Failure
to break the cycle creates the real danger of personal surrender.
There is a limit to the emotional defeat that the human spirit can
absorb. We can muster the personal energy to move forward under
dire circumstances once, maybe twice, but it is increasingly difficult,

a near impossibility, to tackle the same set of crippling circumstances a third time. The likelihood of failure overwhelms the human spirit and we face the real risk of conceding, of going to the corner grocery store for milk and bread, and never coming back.

In the absence of hope, this became a harsh reality for Keith and Debbie. Lacking God's uplifting hand, they searched desperately to fill the incredible emotional void of Rachel's death, with Debbie seeking to replace her and Keith looking for salvation in his professional life.

Not surprisingly, it was not long before they were expecting a baby. Debbie appeared overjoyed, Keith somewhat indifferent. The first band-aid was in place. However, the birth of a healthy baby boy did not replace Rachel. Though Debbie loved him unconditionally and embraced his heart, she could not clothe him in Rachel's beautiful dresses and matching hair bows. Debbie's connection to the past through Rachel's memory and her hope for the future would remain carefully protected in her heart and mind. Keith would smile, stand around the kitchen table with the guys, and pass out "It's a Boy!" cigars, but his behavior appeared remarkably regimented.

Struggling, she and Keith moved forward, trying to keep pace with the rising and setting sun. The burdens of life were written all over their faces. They were living and breathing survival . . . the innocent beauty of Debbie's face was a memory. Keith's robotic engineering nature now appeared to engulf their lives, individually and collectively. Their marriage was on autopilot, and it was drifting off course.

It would not be long before Debbie again happily announced that she was expecting. She was excited at the news that she was going to have a baby girl. Keith displayed the obligatory proud father image. The wound, unhealed with the birth of their son, would get another band-aid. Time, and two healthy children, would not heal their brokenness and emotional bleeding. Life's painful grip would not let go. They would fail to find hope. Debbie and Keith would continue on their course of emotional separation and their marriage would sadly end in divorce.

They crashed into the treetops, just short of the runway. They could see the lights lining the approach in the darkness of the night, but they lacked hope, the fuel of life, to reach their destination safely.

I share their true and painful story that we might see, understand, learn, and protect ourselves from the danger of walking alone. Please know my heart. Though I walked alongside them, I did not walk in their shoes, and I did not suffer their pain. I do not stand in judgment of their decisions. They are wonderful, kind people whom I love. They suffered perhaps the greatest tragedy of life, the loss of their child. Not one of us knows how we would have responded to such pain. However, we should not turn our backs and fail to learn from their nightmare.

In the face of paralyzing pain, our inability to grasp God's promise of hope leaves us drifting in an emotional downward spiral in life's destructive path. Our willpower cannot protect us or transform our heart and soul.

In 1970, facing the potential danger of the Apollo 13 spacecraft deflecting hopelessly away from the earth's atmosphere at the point of reentry, Gene Kranz, the NASA flight director in Houston, Texas, declared, "Failure is not an option." He was committed to success, to a course of action that would guarantee the safe return of the astronauts. His strong statement and the ingenious solution that the mission support team in Houston would devise would not only miraculously save the crew, but would establish a business principle used worldwide. I have personally shown the entire movie to an executive team for the sole purpose of developing a mentality, a mindset of success . . . with failure not seen as an option. It is a motivating story and an effective tool in energizing a team.

Do not be deceived. Do not be blind to the truth—failure in life *is* an option. We face the real possibility of becoming mired in this horrific cycle of misery, the downward spiral of the self-will, seeing our human spirit simply surrender, no longer capable of facing the painful circumstances of life. We simply disappear emotionally. We look for the time-clock of life, hoping to clock out. The decision is ours. God has given us both the gift and the burden of free choice. We have the opportunity to incorporate the presence of God into our decision-making process or go the route of the lone ranger. In God's absence, we drift hopelessly, struggling to gain a sense of direction. In the absence of hope, the anchor for the heartsick soul, failure *is* an option and, in the long term, it is the predictable outcome. I came to fully understand this truth, and I did not learn it in the text of a book.

Failure was knocking at our door. For all practical purposes, I had surrendered. I had given up. Though blinded and drifting aimlessly, I was searching, grasping . . . for someone, for something, for a glimmer of hope, for a lifeline to rescue me. In my weakness and emptiness I groped in darkness, searching for God's hand.

As is our nature, when all else fails, we place the eleventh-hour desperate call to God for help. Figure 4 displays our personal struggle for survival, and our last-ditch effort to seek God's guidance. We have all been there. Despite our best efforts, our circumstances have not improved, and we deem that a call to God can do no harm. We have all sought to negotiate with God, making last-minute promises, seeking God's favor . . . in desperation.

We have already established that God sees our misery, hears our cries for help, and is concerned. He loves us, and this loving God is faithful. God is trustworthy. He honors His covenant with us. His loving, healing hand is displayed throughout the Bible. In the book of Exodus, we see His hand extended to the Israelites, His chosen people, as they wandered in misery in the wilderness. God lifted them up, protected them, saved them. He delivered them with manna from heaven, the vivid picture of His miraculous power. There is no limit to God's love or power.

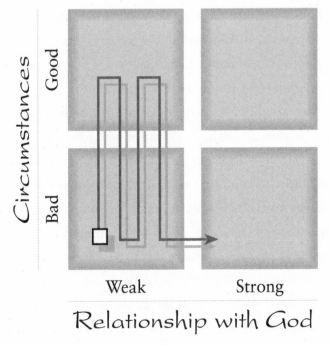

Fig. 4.

I want to be cautious in portraying the image of God and His protective hand. I do not want to create the false impression that an eleventh-hour cry for help automatically results in God's miraculous and instantaneous healing. Nothing could be further from the truth. God's response, His discipline, His spiritual healing, His protection, and His timing are not accidental. God's heart longs to see us grow, develop, and mature spiritually. As we see the hand of God move in our lives, we can be certain that His actions are carefully thought out and orchestrated with fine precision for the sole purpose of enhancing our walk with Him, not for simply intervening to rescue us from our pain.

One of the most insightful, graphic, and beautiful stories in God's Word is found in David's downfall with Bathsheba. It is the perfect picture of man's sin, God's judgment, man's repentance and accountability, and God's forgiveness. Walk closely with me on this journey. You may see our loving God in a new light. This is a spectacular display of God's power and grace.

One evening David simply took a stroll on the rooftop of the palace. From the roof, he saw a beautiful woman, Bathsheba, bathing. Her husband, Uriah, was away at war. King David sent for her, lay with her, and she conceived. He then acted immediately—and independently—to cover his mistake. He quickly retrieved Uriah from the battlefield, that he might lay with his wife. With Uriah thus appearing to be the father of this unborn child, David's error in judgment would be hidden. Uriah, out of respect and honor for his fellow soldiers still on the battlefield, did not comply with David's plan, instead sleeping alone at the gate. Unable to gain Uriah's cooperation, he sent him back to battle with a sealed note for the commander. Under David's specific direction, Uriah was placed on the front line, at the point of fiercest fighting, ensuring his death.

We see the Lord, speaking through the prophet Nathan, confront King David for his sinful actions. The story is found in the twelfth chapter of 2 Samuel. Exposing David in the powerful analogy of the poor man, the Lord challenges David with the truth, "Why did you despise the word of the Lord by doing what is evil in his eyes?" (v. 9). Fully accountable for his actions, the Lord told David that the "sword [would] never depart from [his] house" (v. 10) because he took Uriah's wife. The pain and agony that David would suffer as a result of his actions would be severe. The Lord said:

> Out of your own household I am going to bring calamity upon you. Before your very eyes I will take your wives and give them to one who is close to you, and he will lie with your wives in broad daylight. You did it in secret, but I will do this thing in broad daylight . . . (2 Sam. 12:11–12).

Nathan also said:

> . . . the son born to you will die (2 Sam. 12:14).

When confronted with the truth, David's devastation and despair are painfully evident. He fell before the Lord in Nathan's presence and said, "I have sinned against the Lord" (v. 13). David begged with God for the safety of his infant son, spending sleepless nights on the ground, pleading for God to relent, to reconsider. But, as Paul so clearly conveys in the New Testament, God cannot be mocked. We reap what we sow. David and Bathsheba's baby would die on the seventh day, and David's wives would ultimately be sexually abused in public. This is the biblical story we all know. Many assume it ends there—man sins and God punishes.

This is not the end of the story. In fact, in many ways it is the beginning. Many have failed to read the rest of the story and embrace what is perhaps the most beautiful picture of God in the Old Testament. Yes, David sinned against God and fell from grace, and he was held accountable for his actions. But David's heart was broken, and he fell before the very presence of God, repented, and begged for God's forgiveness. God, in a picture of love and grace that is beyond our grasp, turned the page. Do not miss this . . . God turned the page.

At the sight of King David's brokenness, this magnificent God, our God of incredible love, turned the page, keeping no record of past wrongs. Nathan said to David in the thirteenth verse, "The Lord has taken away your sin." David got up from the ground and worshiped the Lord, forgiven by the grace of God. He comforted his wife Bathsheba, and lay with her. She conceived, and gave birth to a son, and they named him Solomon. The Lord loved him (2 Sam. 12:20, 24). Incredible, absolutely incredible. Solomon, the king whom God loved, the wisest of all of Israel's kings, was the son of David and Bathsheba, the marital union born of adultery and murder.

Many have missed it and have come to believe that the story of David and Bathsheba is solely about man's sin and God's punishment. It is not. It is about man's sin, his heartfelt repentance, and our living, loving God turning the page. Meditate on this for a moment, see God for who He is, and embrace Him.

Make no mistake, there is nothing on earth or in heaven that is beyond the hand, the power, of God. There is no sin, no tragedy, no decision that we can make, no pain that we can possibly incur or inflict that is beyond God's protective and healing hand. Our God is just, fair, and honorable. He disciplines, He loves, and He restores. He turns the page. His loving, protective hand is only a heartbeat away.

Sadly, we seldom approach the living God to rejoice, to worship Him, as King David did. Our basic human nature leads us to seek God only during our greatest misery. Thus, when our circumstances improve (see fig. 5), we characteristically drift away one day at a time.

Again, we find God's Word to be our guide, the great teacher. After the death of King Solomon, his son Rehoboam assumed the throne amidst great difficulty, controversy, and confusion. In time, he stabilized Judah and his position as king was established. Just as we

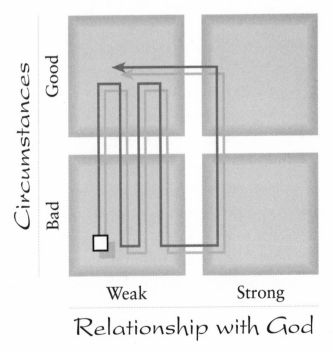

Fig. 5.

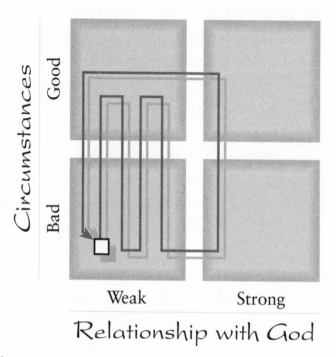

Fig. 6.

see in our own journey, strength in personal circumstances became
his enemy, his Achilles heel, and his downfall. In the twelfth chapter
of 2 Chronicles, it is not difficult to see ourselves, our basic nature,
in his story, "After . . . he had become strong, he and all Israel with
him abandoned the law of the Lord. . . . He did evil because he had
not set his heart on seeking the Lord"(vv. 1, 14). That is our risk, our
great risk. Strengthened and stabilized, we abandon God's council.

We tend to have short memories. Our last-minute negotia-
tions with God—"God, if you will rescue me this time, I promise
I will . . . "—are generally forgotten. I have been there. You probably
have too. This joyous moment, the time in which we are bathed in
wonderful circumstances of life and are experiencing a deep,
meaningful walk with God, is difficult to maintain. Ironically, this

moment of ecstasy again places us at the greatest risk of all, a strong dose of pride buoyed by great circumstances in life, and we tend to drift. Often, the initial deterioration goes unnoticed, even to us. Our external shell is soundly in place. Most often, *invisible risk* rears its ugly head, and we gradually drift away from our short-lived loving relationship with the Lord.

In the course of time, we experience Rehoboam's fate, and deterioration, destruction, and despair follow. We have come full circle (see fig. 6), and we find ourselves again facing difficult circumstances . . . with an absent God. It is our basic nature. We should not be blind to the fact that our cyclical behavior is reflective of our spiritual heritage. The following abbreviated version of the ninth chapter of Nehemiah is a snapshot of our spiritual forefathers, wandering in the wilderness, living out the Human Cycle, circling the racetrack of life, again and again.

You are the Lord God, who chose Abram . . .

you made a covenant with him . . .

You saw the suffering of our forefathers in Egypt . . .

You divided the sea before them . . .

By day you led them with a pillar of cloud,

and by night with a pillar of fire . . .

you spoke to them from heaven . . .

In their hunger you gave them bread from heaven

and in their thirst you brought them water from the rock . . .

But they . . . became arrogant and stiff-necked . . .

They refused to listen and failed to remember . . .

they were disobedient and rebelled against you . . .

So you handed them over to their enemies . . .

But when they were oppressed they cried out to you.

From heaven you heard them and . . . rescued them . . .

But as soon as they were at rest, they . . . did . . . evil . . .

And when they cried out to you again, you heard . . .

and . . . you delivered them time after time

(Neh. 9:7–9, 11–13, 15–17, 26–28).

This repetitive cycle of success and failure eventually wears down the human spirit and we surrender. Paul, in the tenth chapter of 1 Corinthians, gives us tremendous spiritual guidance and warns us as we reflect upon the struggle of our spiritual forefathers:

. . . I do not want you to be ignorant of the fact, brothers,

that our forefathers were all under the cloud and that they

all passed through the [floodwaters of the Red] sea. . . .

They all ate the same spiritual food and drank the same

spiritual drink . . . from the spiritual rock . . .

and that rock was Christ.

Nevertheless, God was not pleased with most of them . . .

[and] scattered [them] over the desert.

Now these things occurred as examples

to keep us from setting our hearts on evil things as they did. . . .

These things happened to them as examples

and were written down as warnings for us . . .

So, if you think you are standing firm,

be careful that you don't fall! (vv. 1, 3–6, 11–12).

Thus, God's Word provides living examples, and He warns us of "standing firm" without Him. The Bible, this large, mystical, complex book about ancient times, is, in fact, God's message for us, and it is extraordinarily clear. Paul wants to make certain that we know. He speaks directly to us and cautions us. Those who went before us actually witnessed God's vivid presence as revealed in His protective miracles—the parting of the Red Sea and water overflowing from the desert rock; yet our forefathers still drifted away. The Bible rests in our hands. We have every opportunity to gain knowledge, to embrace God at a very personal level, and to prevent history from repeating itself . . . to see God as the author of hope.

And yet, we struggle. We carry God's Word comfortably in our hands, but very few of us have developed a deep enough relationship with the Lord to trust Him when the stakes are high . . . to trust Him with everything, to trust Him with our broken hearts.

We live by our feelings, not by our faith. Tragic circumstances like ours, and Debbie and Keith's, make it more visible, more evident. We get on the racetrack of life, the Human Cycle, and we cannot get off. We simply do not trust God enough to give Him complete control when we face painful circumstances. We spend a lifetime oscillating between dependence on ourselves and God . . . and we are addicted to it. It is all we know. We fail to reach out to God and we miss His healing hand, His grace.

Life is difficult, and pain is a certainty of life. We have all suffered. We have all seen and felt paralyzing pain in our very midst. Yet, life does not bestow us with the innate gift of freeing ourselves from the crippling emotional impact of its suffering. As we have seen together, *unawareness* and *invisible risk*, our naïve spiritual innocence and our basic lone-ranger lifestyle of independence from God, have put us in great jeopardy, without a lifeline. Our failure to grasp the person of God, the living God, the loving God, the God who turns the page, has left us without hope in life's downward emotional cycle of despair. In our blindness and all-consuming misery, we have failed to see, to realize, to know that God provides a way out.

God's promise gives us the assurance of a spiritual lifeline. In the words of the contemporary song by Don Moen, "God will make a way where there seems to be no way." These words were written for such a moment as this.

In the tenth chapter of 1 Corinthians, Paul conveys God's promise of hope. In the thirteenth verse, he shares:

> . . . God is faithful; he will not let you be tempted beyond what you can bear. But when your are tempted, he will also provide a way out so that you can stand up under it.

In the midst of a living personal hell, with the walls of life crashing, I never dreamed that suffering—such overwhelming pain—could so richly embody the presence of God. I never imagined that my weakness, my surrender, would open the door for God Himself to walk in, to provide a way out.

CHAPTER FIVE

Strength in Weakness

*"Though I have fallen,
I will rise.
Though I sit in darkness,
the Lord will be my light."*
—Micah 7:8

I ronically, human weakness, our independent willpower and the absence of God, provides one of the greatest opportunities for God to reveal Himself.

Indeed, in Jesus' words to Paul, ". . . my power is made perfect in [your] weakness" (2 Cor. 12:9). To protect Paul from pride and conceit, Jesus placed a burden upon him beyond his ability to manage. Paul, in his weakness, would seek God's power of protection. Paul grew to delight in his weakness, realizing that hardship and difficulties of life caused him to grow in the strength of God's grace (2 Cor. 12:7–10).

This would prove to be my story, my life's experience. After years of independently juggling my successes and failures in life, God gave me more than I could handle. God knew, and I would painfully learn, that He required my attention, my full and undivided attention, if I was to grow into His presence and experience His grace.

It is not the American way to delight in weakness. In fact, our society teaches the exact opposite. Be strong, be independent, chart your own course, prove yourself, and my favorite—eat what you kill. Yet, Paul's words in 2 Corinthians have hidden insight.

When we are strong, we are bulletproof.
At our point of greatest weakness, we are vulnerable.
When we are vulnerable, we listen.
When we listen, we learn.
When we learn, we grow.

If you have teenage children, this will ring true. Weakness and vulnerability open the ears to hear.

In my weakness, the dawning of a new day began. I have no recollection of the exact date, but I vividly remember the despair. Late one morning, I decided to leave the office and spend my lunchtime in the sanctuary of our church. I was not going with the intent of sharing time with the Lord. I was searching, searching in the darkness for hope, someone, something to piece together my future, the rest of my life. En route, my mind drifted to the minister of families at our church.

The Bible speaks of God's angels. Gayle Haywood is one of those special people—selfless in her love, tireless in her efforts, a woman with God's heart. We should have eyes to see and ears to hear, for God places His angels in our midst.

I thought, *Oh, how I would love to see her, to talk with her;* but, the chance of that happening with no advance notice was remote. I would just go to the sanctuary and sit. I parked in the virtually empty north lot, went in the side entrance, and walked in facing the church receptionist. She was talking to Gayle . . . God's simple grace. I spent the next hour in Gayle's office. I once heard that "if you don't know where you are going, you will probably get there." That is essentially what happened. I rambled from one dark moment of my life to the next, and she spent her time attempting to prop me up.

As I prepared to leave, Gayle prayed. The memory of this moment is vivid. She spoke personally and lovingly to God. This God she was talking to was present. She was talking with Him, and I sensed He was listening. Her connection was a local call, and I had believed all along that God was long distance. The connection Gayle had with the Lord was foreign to me. I listened attentively, somewhat puzzled, but emotionally searching. I knew that I needed to understand what she felt in her heart. I thanked her for her time, and as I stood up to leave, she asked if I had read the book *Secrets of the Vine* by Bruce Wilkinson. I had not, but ironically I had recently spoken with a friend in Oklahoma City who had recommended it. Gayle gave me a copy, and over the next few days, I read it.

First, the book spoke of unconfronted sin and God's discipline. It didn't take a rocket scientist to understand that concept. That was all about the chess player on high moving pawns on the board, and I was already in that game. Next, the author presented the concept of producing spiritual fruit and of God's pruning, and that made common sense. The part that left me curious was his discussion about "abiding" with Christ. He stated that surveys of Christians indicated that only 5 percent of Christians abide. Honestly, I didn't know what he meant by abiding, and I dismissed it.

Although my spiritual journey, my search for hope, lacked clarity, focus, and understanding of the person of God, His promise would prove true. God was watching, listening, and waiting patiently for me to open my heart, not just my mind. Unbeknownst to me, God was at work. I was beginning to get glimpses of Him, and He was silently laying the groundwork to change my life. This previously distant God of mine was close. My life was dismantled; like Paul, my heart had "felt the sentence of death." My success, my pride, my fall, my despair . . . had all been beautifully and painfully experienced, in order that I might surrender "self" and embrace this loving, living God. The wheels were in motion.

In the absence of my spiritual leadership in the family, God was present. My first glimpse of Him came in the power of His protective hand. Amber, our middle child, was mired in those incredibly difficult teenage years. For this season of life, Jeannie and I were emotionally paralyzed, and struggled to give her the parental support she needed. Having lived through those difficult years with her older siblings, Staci and Dustin, I was honestly afraid for her safety. She was going it alone, or so I thought. She blazed through, sidestepping one land mine after another. She came out of the fog, and she blossomed beautifully.

For the first time in my life, I had seen the very presence of God's hand, and I was certain of it. I bought a card and wrote Amber a long note, speaking of God's protective hand. I did not want her to miss it. She had a gift that none of her siblings had received. I told her to treasure it, hold it near to her heart, and share it with others. God Himself had stepped in and protected her. I did not understand it, but I knew God had intervened. I could see it.

Do not miss this point—we have evolved to dismiss God's presence if we do not see Him part the Red Sea, raise the dead, or turn water into wine. As Elihu spoke to Job, he painted a wonderfully accurate image of how God speaks to us today, in our very lives.

> For God does speak—now one way, now another—though man may not perceive it. In a dream, in a vision of the night, when deep sleep falls on men as they slumber in their beds, he may speak in their ears and terrify them with warnings, to turn man from wrongdoing and keep him from pride, to preserve his soul . . . (Job 31:14–18).

When we do not see "the burning bush," we simply overlook God's presence. What I had never understood, I was beginning to see, up close and in person. As the Scripture passage above so aptly says, "For God does speak—now one way, now another. . . ." I stopped and looked, somewhat in awe, at the very presence of God in the face of our daughter.

At this moment, God had revealed Himself to me and I knew it, but I was still months away from seeing the heart of God, from feeling His presence.

I had no idea that He . . . felt sorrow for the Israelites as they wandered.

that He . . . heard when they cried out at the Red Sea.

that He . . . felt my pain.

I did not realize that He . . . saw,

that He . . . hurt,

that He . . . loved.

God is a God of feelings and emotions, and I did not know it. He was concerned when His chosen people wandered in the wilderness, and now, He felt the same pain for us. He suffered as we struggled.

And then, in a moment, after a long painful journey in the valley of the shadow of death, my world began to change. At first it seemed relatively insignificant. Gayle stopped me in the hall at church and asked if I would teach *Secrets of the Vine* on Sunday nights in the fall of 2001. The decision I made would alter my course and change my life in ways that I could never have imagined. I protested, just as Moses protested to God in the fourth chapter of Exodus, that she should find someone else. Gayle told me that she really believed that I was the right person to teach. The Lord gave her spiritual insight into my life, and I am thankful for her receptivity to the voice of God and for her obedience. I pray that my heart will grow to be like hers.

I had a lot of respect for Gayle, so I accepted. Four months later, before the end of the year, I would get my first taste of the living God.

CHAPTER SIX

The Dawn of a New Day

". . . the people living in darkness
have seen a great light;
on those living in the land of
the shadow of death
a light has dawned."
—Matthew 4:16

The journey of independence, my reliance on personal will and determination, had ended. I started anew, with a mere glimpse of "this God" that had suffered *with* our family. I would come to grasp His presence. The Bible says that Moses, despite great trials, "persevered because he saw him who is invisible"(Heb. 11:27). In the months to come, I too, would see Him.

It was time to teach. I reread *Secrets of the Vine*, studied corresponding Scripture, and prepared. I could teach, and I looked forward to an audience. I had a flair for the stage. Though I had never shared it with anyone, I was disappointed at the lack of a crowd. We had consistent attendance of about six people.

The first several Sunday nights were enjoyable, but not overly eventful. The group bonded nicely, and I, in my usual style, displayed personal vulnerability. I told the class that Gayle Haywood had asked me to teach because I was the poster child of the first chapter—unbridled sin and God's discipline. My comment, delivered for effect and humor, was successful. My comfort in my vulnerability was based on my long-standing high self-esteem, and in no way reflected a desire to display God's grace. I breezed through the first six or seven chapters with ease. I was enjoying teaching, and those who attended seemed truly touched.

If you detect familiarity, you are accurate. Though God was actively at work in my life, "I" was still comfortably in charge . . . same song, second verse. As we neared the end of the book, I faced this dilemma of "abiding with Christ." Remember, the survey said that only 5 percent of Christians abide. I did not really understand the concept of abiding, but I knew that I was not in that elite group. With ego remarkably still fully intact, I told the class that this was uncharted water for me. I taught the material, and presented those mysterious concepts about (1) God wanting more time with us, not more from us, and (2) miraculous multiplication.

To make matters more complicated for me, the author recommended *daily* time with the Lord, with a commitment to prayer, reading the Bible, and journaling. Despite my mistakes in life, my upbringing taught me to color inside the lines, so I, out of a sense of obligation, bought and distributed journals. We had one class left, so I suggested that we take the remaining seven days to give each of us a kick start in our daily walk with the Lord. I was functioning on pure, 100 percent obligatory oxygen. Unbeknownst to the class, this was like being held hostage for me. I did not have one disciplined bone in my body when it came to studying God's Word. Anything, any task, that required more than about three consecutive days, was beyond me. Repetition was a frightening thought.

Now, for you to fully appreciate my misery, I will share a personal story. Many of you will cringe. Years ago, Jeannie asked me to put up a chair railing and picture molding in our formal living room. I am a handyman, so this posed no problem. With excitement, I recalled my algebra, designed, measured, and made my hardware store run. I eagerly located the studs, maneuvered around the electrical outlets, and completed the work on the wall adjacent to the kitchen. I puttied nail holes, caulked, stood back, and admired my work. Though I do not remember, I am certain that I called Jeannie in to pat me on the back for my great work. Days, weeks, months passed. She asked, pleaded, and ultimately begged me to do the other three walls. In total boredom, I ultimately did it. I would have rather taken a beating.

Thus, you can imagine my anxiety about the forthcoming daily routine. I had backed myself into a corner. I was teaching, leading the class. It was my responsibility to set an example. In seven days, I would have to face people that had become my friends. Surely, now bearing this burden of being the teacher, I could muster the necessary discipline for a week to set the right example and avoid total humiliation. Day two of my journal started with, "November 27, 2001 (Day #2) —I really don't feel like doing this today." That is the absolute truth; I have the journal to prove it. I survived the seven days, and proudly shared my success with the class. I had reached the finish line, or so I thought.

We finished our last class with a round of warm hugs for newfound friends. Julia Dunn, a sweet woman of God whom I have come to love, told me that she had recommended to Gayle that we repeat the class in the winter. I smiled graciously and said nothing, but I thought *Oh, no!*

I kept reading my Bible and journaling every day, just in case Gayle asked. Not knowing where to start, I just jumped into Romans. I had taught Romans one time, so it seemed non-threatening. Genesis 1:1? Not a chance. The Old Testament, with the chronology "of all time," and Leviticus (if I remembered correctly), full of law after law, didn't interest me. Furthermore, Exodus had the Ten Commandments, and I knew what was there. The New Testament would be the path of least resistance. I read my Bible every day. I was punching the spiritual clock.

I was cautiously looking over my shoulder, expecting to hear from Gayle. I did not have to wait long. Gayle, her warm smile glowing, told me she had received excellent feedback from the class, and asked if I would teach again beginning in January. Those were her words, almost verbatim, so appropriately stated. What I heard was, "They loved you," and my ego greatly appreciated it. I had long since fallen from my pedestal as the perfect dad; work, while challenging, was not fulfilling; and my marriage was barely surviving from day to day. *They wanted me!* How could I say no? I couldn't. I would have to continue daily Bible reading and journaling, but it was worth it. It only required a few minutes a day, and I was willing to pay the price.

A few days before Christmas, something unexpected happened— something incredible, something unexplainable. My obligatory, regimented time of reading and writing disappeared. I felt drawn into God's presence. With His heart giving light to my path, I opened the Bible and read, with fifteen minutes growing into an hour, or longer. My date-driven journaling became words that reflected the spiritual longing of my heart. God, the chess player on high, suddenly felt very close. The winds of change, deep within my soul, were real.

Internally, silently, in my own world, I tried to make sense of it.

Though I have spent my entire professional career in the health-care industry, I have the mindset of an engineer. Rational, logical thinking has always prevailed. It has been my foundation for decision making. This intangible "God thing," real as it was, was mystifying. I continued, Day Nineteen, Day Twenty, and Day Twenty-One. I had enjoyed a part-time relationship with God for my entire adult life, and now He was moving in.

But this God, this mysterious living God, would prove to be as visible, just as real, as the memory I have of Jeannie and me, years earlier, sitting at the kitchen table on a Saturday afternoon, discussing how to tell the children we were going to get a divorce. To this day, I can still hear my heartbeat exploding in my ears. It is as if it were yesterday. God would grow to be equally vivid in my heart and mind, and it would not be long before I began to see Him in my daily walk. The downward, emotionally depleting spiral of self-sufficiency, just basic human nature, was broken. I did not fully understand the implications, but I knew it was a new day.

If this moment causes you to pause, to consider putting this book aside, to go read something more practical and believable, to go watch television, or to go run an errand, I understand. If you had shared this story with me at an earlier time in my life, I would have smiled graciously, pretended to have a receptive heart, and immediately begun looking for a polite way to leave. The next time you called for lunch, I would have been busy. I might have gone and put up chair railing and picture molding on those other three walls of the living room. It would have been a very attractive alternative.

All humor aside, there is a critical point, a golden nugget, embedded in this moment that I do not want you to miss. I truly did not know that God could emerge from the fog and reveal Himself to me. I did not expect it. Somewhat blindly, with the guidance of God's invisible hand, I had simply, honestly begun walking "in His path." Too often, we choose a course to "find Him." We plan our work, we work our plan, and we are mystified that God is not there. I am convinced that we should focus less and less on serving and obeying, and focus more and more on devoting our hearts and souls to simply "seeking the Lord" (1 Chron. 22:19). The book of Matthew, in the words of Paul Harvey, tells "the rest of the story." "Seek [God] first . . . and all these things will be given to you as well" (6:33).

My incredible, unexplainable experience is not really that amazing. I was calmly walking in His path, and He lifted me up. It is not some mysterious event revealed by some magical God on high. It is quite simple. We, the people of God, walking in His presence, experience His grace.

That is exactly where I was, in His path, with a new song in my heart.

CHAPTER SEVEN

A New Song

"I waited patiently for the Lord;
he turned to me and heard my cry.
He lifted me out of the slimy pit,
out of the mud and the mire;
he set my feet on a rock
and gave me a firm place to stand.
He put a new song in my mouth,
a hymn of praise to our God."
—Psalm 40:1–3

It quickly became a weekend routine for me to be sitting in the corner coffee shop parking lot when they opened . . . 6:00 A.M. on Saturdays and 6:30 A.M. on Sundays. It was my time with God. I looked forward to that first cup of coffee, and I thirsted for God's Word, my private time with Him. In my journey through God's Word, I would come to Psalm 63, and I would feel David's heart when he wrote, "O God . . . earnestly I seek you; my soul thirsts for you . . . " (v. 1). My spiritual world of *unawareness* was melting away, and the long-distance God of my past had been replaced.

Bruce Wilkinson's concept of miraculous multiplication, so foreign to me just three months earlier, would be revealed in living color. In the eighth chapter of *Secrets of the Vine*, he states that God wants more time with us, not more good works from us. He suggests that spending more time with God, living in His presence—abiding—will miraculously multiply the opportunities to be of service for God. They did not teach miraculous multiplication in calculus or probability and statistics at Georgia Tech, and it seemed irrational to my engineering mind. But I would soon see the miraculous mathematician at work—from the coffee shop on Sunday morning to forty thousand feet above the face of the earth.

In February of 2002, a man standing over my right shoulder preparing his coffee asked if I was a preacher. I sheepishly smiled and said, "No, I have just started reading the Bible every day." I told him that my spiritual walk had always been intellectual; that I had never consistently read the Bible. He briefly shared a similar spiritual heritage, smiled warmly, and left. I wrote in my journal, "God, please bring him back next Sunday." The next Sunday morning he walked in, walked directly to where I was sitting, and said, "I hoped that you would be here." Those were his words, verbatim. I smiled and said, "I hoped that you would come." He fixed his coffee, stood in front of me, and leaned against the window. We talked for ten or fifteen minutes, expanding on our prior conversation about this intellectual walk with the Lord and the importance of spending time daily with God. As he turned to leave, he looked back, extended his hand, and said, "My name is Steven. I'll see you next Sunday." Steven sat down the next Sunday and he and I have spent virtually every Sunday morning together since that day. We have experienced the Lord together.

I share the details of my journey with Steven for two reasons. First, God simply walked him into my life, and second, it began to happen regularly. I will never forget a flight from Nashville to Dallas where a flight attendant kneeled in the aisle with her elbows propped on my armrest, talking about her intellectual spiritual upbringing and her need to be in God's Word. She was in her mid-thirties, brought up in the church, had never read her Bible, and felt disconnected from God. She was right there, just inches from my face, for the last twenty minutes of the flight, getting up periodically to let passengers go by. I shared my heart with her. I was just minding my own business, spending time privately with the Lord, as He was walking people into my life. I was amazed.

Our son, Dustin, was standing in our kitchen a few days later, and I was telling him of the remarkable events that continued to take place in my everyday life. I looked and sounded like a child with a new toy. He said, and I quote, "Dad, it's going to happen to you all the time." And it did. As my amazement ceased, my spiritual joy was growing, day by day.

I continued to read the New Testament every day, Romans, 1 Corinthians, 2 Corinthians, Galatians, and Ephesians. I grew fond of Paul and wanted to read about his life, so I went to the book of Acts. I came to the twenty-sixth chapter, the sixteenth verse. It would be an awakening experience, giving me such incredible spiritual insight and deeply altering my understanding of my responsibility to God. Paul, defending himself before King Agrippa, reflected upon his conversion experience with Jesus on the road to Damascus. After Jesus had knocked him off of his feet and temporarily blinded him, Jesus had said to Saul (Paul), "Now get up and stand on your feet. I have appeared to you to appoint you as a servant and as a witness of what you have seen of me and what I will show you." That was Jesus' message to Paul, and it was God's direction for me, to be "servant" and "witness" of what God had shown me.

Unbelievable! In my conservative upbringing I had come to believe that my primary responsibilities were perfect attendance in Sunday school and Friday night youth visitation. I thought God was keeping a spiritual scorecard, and I had years of perfect attendance pins, seven or eight as I recall. We even attended church when we vacationed, to keep my record intact. I thought I would be judged on production. I had been wrong, terribly wrong. God did not want "production"; He wanted my heart. As I now know, He possesses the mathematical formula for miraculous multiplication. If He had my heart, the glory of His presence would follow, and His grace would overflow exponentially. He had given me gifts, painful gifts, and He wanted me to share them. That was it. That was all. That was the whole story . . . spiritually rich, spiritually fulfilling, and yet so simple. As Paul so beautifully and accurately conveyed in the first chapter of 2 Corinthians:

> We were under great pressure, far beyond our ability to endure, so that we despaired even of life. Indeed, in our hearts we felt the sentence of death. But this happened that we might not rely on ourselves but on God . . . (vv. 8–9).

> . . . the Father of compassion and the God of all comfort, who comforts us in all our troubles, so that we can comfort those in any trouble with the comfort we ourselves have received from God (vv. 3–4).

What was happening to me was not a new concept. God, in His infinite wisdom, had always given painful gifts, that we might grow to depend on Him, know His heart, share His love, and find joy and spiritual fullness in Him.

This is very powerful and it speaks to each of us. Look closely at the fourth verse. God intervenes for a greater purpose . . . His purpose. His protective hand is not there solely to rescue us. He is committed to comfort us, but He also desires to teach us, so that we are prepared and equipped to share His love and spiritual insight with others who face similar struggles in life. Then, when we see their pain, we understand, we truly understand. The challenges they face in life, we have faced. We have more than sympathy . . . we have empathy. Suddenly, we are standing alongside Saul (Paul) on the road to Damascus, and we understand. God gives us the opportunity and responsibility to simply share what He has shown us, taught us, and revealed to us individually in our personal journeys through life. God places people along our paths whom we can support, guide, and minister to spiritually. The heart of God rests with us in the very presence of the Holy Spirit. We are no longer alone.

I have vivid recollection of the Great Commission being taught again and again in church when I was a teenager. It was our challenge, our responsibility as Christians. I was in awe:

Therefore go and make disciples of all nations, baptizing them in the name of the Father and of the Son and of the Holy Spirit, and teaching them to obey everything I have commanded you (Matt. 28:19–20).

I was overwhelmed. I did not know where to start. Going to "all nations, baptizing them," and "teaching them to obey everything," was a daunting task. Like every other young teenager, I memorized the Great Commission . . . and that was it. I share that experience not to make light of it, for it is a great truth, but rather to bring our daily walk with God into focus. As He did with Saul (Paul), God has given us the responsibility of being "servant and . . . witness of what [we] have seen of [Him], and what [He] will show [us]" (Acts 26:16).

This is a fascinating insight. Each of us has had unique experiences in life, and has experienced God in remarkably different ways in our respective journeys. God has taught us many different things. My individual responsibility, your individual responsibility, is not to canvass the entire world, making disciples of all people in all nations. It is our responsibility to grow into the presence of God and share His love and spiritual insight with everyone He places in our paths. Thus, we collectively reach all the nations with God's love, one person at a time.

There is one more truth, a great spiritual insight that we must grasp, before we move on in our journey together. So often, the very thought of sharing God's love is intimidating and overwhelming. The spiritual picture that I have just painted is freeing. No longer are we faced with the overwhelming task of knowing all things for all people. We now are only accountable for sharing that which God has revealed to us, information that rests within our soul. Share what God has given you, and thirst for more. Broaden your knowledge, broaden your horizons, and experience pure joy. As Bruce Wilkinson explains in *The Prayer of Jabez,* when Jabez cried out to God and asked that God "enlarge his territory," this is exactly what he meant. God, show me more . . . give me more.

My eyes were opened. It was suddenly crystal clear why God had allowed Steven to walk into my life, and a flight attendant to do the unthinkable, simply kneel in the aisle, allowing the world to stand still. God had revealed Himself to me, shown me, taught me, and I had something to share.

Now I understood, and God was beginning to impact my actions, my thoughts, and my heart. The change in my actions and thoughts did not surprise me; the fact that my relationship with Him was changing my heart and my character shocked me. I almost couldn't believe it. 1 Corinthians 13, the chapter about God's love, was taking on new meaning. "Love is patient, love is kind . . . it is not proud" (v. 4), was not just intended for a Sunday morning sermon. It was about God's heart—and mine. In the spirit of David's guidance to Solomon and the Israelites in 1 Chronicles 22:19, I was beginning to "devote [my] heart and soul to seeking the Lord [my] God." The winds of change were blowing strong.

When I came upon Job's final chapter, his personal conversation with the Lord, I knew what he meant when he spoke to God and said, "My ears had heard of you but now my eyes have seen you" (42:5). God's protection of Amber, my meeting Steven at the coffee shop, and my time with the flight attendant were all such a display of God's presence. That which I had never seen, I now could not deny. It was just the beginning. Dustin had said, "Dad, it's going to happen to you all the time." He was right.

Well into the winter class of *Secrets of the Vine*, I had found new energy, new purpose, and new insight. Now, I was more than the poster child for unbridled sin. I had much more to share. We had a great time in the Lord.

I charged through Day One Hundred with the Lord on cruise control. The unimaginable was happening. Initially afraid of being able to survive the seven-day kick-off with our first class, I was breezing. I finished Acts, and transitioned with great comfort and heartfelt desire to Genesis 1:1. Nine months later, I would study the twenty-second chapter of Revelation and complete my first journey through the entire Bible. The Bible that I had carried in my childhood always seemed so big and complex. I had never dared to purchase a one-year Bible or consider such a daunting task. It suddenly seemed small and clear. I would finish Revelation 22:21 one morning, and start Genesis 1:1 anew the next day.

My spiritual journey was euphoric, and it was effortless. As I have reflected and shared these first one hundred days with you, I have attempted, with the written word, to let you feel my heartbeat. It was true joy. People like Steven continued to walk into my life, and I was able to share the presence of God. I studied on airplanes, studied in restaurants when traveling, and I had my regular table at the coffee shop on the weekend. Gregory, a newfound friend at the coffee shop, invited Jeannie and me over for dinner. His wife, Kelly, whom I had never met, referred to me as "the Bible man" . . . hysterical! I was on a journey from the "valley of the shadow of death" to "the Bible man"; who would have ever believed it?

Who would believe that there is such a path in life—from the sinful heartbreak of adultery, the doorstep of divorce, to "the Bible man"? Our journey through life causes us to stop, ask this very question of ourselves, and we become paralyzed. We write ourselves off. Surely . . . surely God could not use someone who has done what I have done, who knows what I know, who thinks what I think, or who is as old as I am, or who _____. Just fill in the blank yourself. We all have our own personal stories, our own excuses. Not one of us is perfect. No one has stayed on God's straight and narrow path. Yet, as I shared earlier in this chapter, God gives us the gift of sharing and supporting where He Himself has comforted and taught us.

The Bible speaks powerfully throughout. A simple glimpse of Abraham and Sarah becoming the parents of Isaac well after their childbearing years, and Jesus' conversion of Saul (Paul), the great persecutor of Christians, on the road to Damascus, is all the support we need to dismiss our excuses, stand up, and be counted. My journey from the valley of the shadow of death to "the Bible man," and subsequently, "the coffee shop chaplain," was living proof for me. The same truth applies in your life. The Bible, God's Living Word, has spoken. Let us have ears to hear and hearts to understand.

People approached me all the time. It was so effortless. I was doing just what the Lord directed Paul to do. I accepted our God-given responsibility of being a "servant and . . . witness" to the things He had shown me (Acts 26:16). I was going in the right direction.

I was recovering rapidly in the eyes of the children. It is a known fact that children can overcome almost any parental mistake, and love will survive. A psychiatrist who followed the O. J. Simpson trial said that his children would still love him, even if the truth revealed that he had killed their mother. That is powerful. I found it to be absolutely true.

But there was another storm gathering on the horizon, and I did not see it. I highly suspect that you, the reader, may have already detected it. It's a storm you may have experienced. Everybody I worked with and came into contact with detected my spiritual journey. It was unmistakable. I was breathing it. Sadly, I had relegated Jeannie and the children to being mere spectators. They saw my energy, my spiritual cup overflowing, but I did not invite them in. Jeannie, understandably deeply scarred, had serious doubts about the validity of my story.

Unaware and unintentionally, with pride still having a real impact on my life, I had excluded them.

In addition, for the first time in my professional life, I was traveling every week, wheels up at 6:00 A.M. Monday morning, touchdown at 11:50 P.M. Thursday night, packing a suitcase on Sunday afternoon, and teaching at church on Sunday night. I was personally engaged, but my schedule and my spiritual detachment were taking a toll on our family. Stress fractures, cracks in the family armor, were still present and the pressure was building.

I have clear recollection of a quarterly medical staff meeting in the spring of 2002 in one of our hospitals in Salt Lake City where the guest speaker was a state representative who was CEO of the Utah Boys Ranch. As the meeting got underway, my cell phone rang three times in about fifteen minutes, conflict on the home front. I was juggling . . . with no success.

After giving a legislative update, the guest speaker went into his fund-raising pitch. He introduced two clean-cut young men who told their individual success stories. They had been shipped off to the Boys Ranch, a boot-camp environment for out-of-control teenagers. One young man from Dallas, Texas, shared that he grew up in a family of five children. His dad had traveled five days a week, and he told a spine-tingling story of family and personal deterioration. I looked for someone to pull the knife out of my back.

Afterwards, I stood in the hallway outside of the cafeteria and talked with the CEO of the hospital, a subordinate and dear Christian friend. He knew of my deep commitment to my family, and he saw me struggling to balance travel demands and personal responsibilities. He looked me straight in the face, smiled warmly, and told me I would be gone in six weeks. He would prove to be wrong—he missed it by a couple of months.

I called the CEO of our company in April, we announced in May, and I worked my last day in July. The political complexity of the corporate world and its suffocating travel demands had created a sense of urgency that would give me God-given peace as I walked away.

CHAPTER EIGHT

Four-Part Harmony

". . . I will show love to the house of Judah;
and I will save them—not by bow,
sword or battle, or by horses and
horsemen, but by the Lord their God."
—Hosea 1:7

The birth of spring left the starkness of winter behind, the blooming tulips by the mailbox seemingly more beautiful than in years past. Perhaps it had been several years since I had noticed. I was teaching Philip Yancey's book *What's So Amazing About Grace* at church, and I recorded my two hundredth consecutive day with the Lord. The impact of bombs dropping, once a common occurrence in our home, now seemed but a distant memory. For the first time in years, I could stand on the patio in the warmth of the afternoon and breathe peace.

In the eye of the storm, on a day when the whole world was collapsing, our family counselor had given me sound advice, "Don't look beyond your headlights." Those headlights, which had once shown no further than the next sunrise of life, now beamed into the distance. For the first time in years, I remembered that life had once been joyful. I knew we had not arrived, for spiritual growth is found in the journey, not the destination; but I could see again. That which had once appeared impossible could now be heard . . . the faint heartbeat of our marriage, beating softly. I could see a miracle unfolding before my very eyes, and I knew I was not alone, "The . . . Lord is my strength . . . he enables me to go on the heights" (Hab. 3:19).

The summer of 2002 brought wedding bells for Dustin and his bride, Amy. Beautiful pictures would create memories of smiling faces, forever frozen in time. The image of our family, fully intact, was the artwork of the living God.

The wedding, for all its beauty, was painful for Jeannie, who lovingly gave her son to Amy. Jeannie, in giving, felt the pain of losing the man in her life from whom she felt the greatest love. That truth was evident in her soft tears as Dustin said, "I do." She endured that emptiness and the personal wars she was fighting within her soul for another six months until, miraculously, we would begin to drink from God's fountain together.

No longer traveling, I began to help Jamie, the store manager, open the coffee shop every weekday morning at 5:30 A.M.—I was often his first customer. My three hundredth consecutive day with the Lord would be uneventful, as normal as breathing. My coffee shop "ministry" would continue, as the Lord led wonderful people into my life. In addition to visiting with Steven on Sunday mornings, I had met a man named Dan Parks several months earlier. Our introduction began like almost every other, with amazing consistency. He stood over my right shoulder and chatted briefly about my reading the Bible. He moved in front of me and leaned against the window the next time we talked. We connected at a spiritual level before he ever sat down. At this moment, I can still see him move his hand from his head to his heart the first time he described his spiritual journey. He had come to know the Lord at an entirely different level through an incredibly painful experience. We began to talk almost every weekday. Dan was the operations manager for a communications company. That irrelevant fact would prove amazing, miraculous in its own right. His company's business relationship with a local publisher would give birth to the concept of the book *Painful Gifts*.

Miraculous multiplication, once mystifying to me, was now commonplace in my life. I did not understand it the first time I read it, and I did not believe it the first time I taught it. Now, I was living it. Not once—not once—in this journey had I asked God to give me the opportunity to share His love, the gift He had given me. And yet it continued to happen all the time. I was in His path.

Nowhere was it more cherished than in our own family. Megan, our youngest daughter, is a young lady with a beautiful spirit. I stopped by the high school one day to see a teacher of hers who had visited Israel and had pictures of Jerusalem. As I met him for the first time, he shook my hand firmly, looked directly into my eyes, and said, "Megan has told me about your walk with the Lord." He had never met me, and the only thing he knew about me was that I loved the Lord. Megan told him. The same little girl who stood in the shadow of the night, her finger on the pulse of an impending divorce, now opened her eyes to the reality, the very presence of God.

Megan, without us knowing, had been looking into participating in a church mission trip to Amsterdam in December. Awesome, just awesome.

Staci, our oldest daughter, is married to Chris, a Presbyterian youth minister on Hilton Head Island. (Tough duty, but somebody has to do it!) Staci, frighteningly like her dad when it comes to being in control, called me in December and said, "Dad, I know I'm way behind you, but I wanted you to know that today is my thirtieth consecutive day spending time in God's Word." As I talked with her on the phone, I wiped tears from my cheeks. Later, on the one hundredth day of her journey in God's Word, His very presence, she sent me an e-mail that said:

> So how pumped are you for me . . . Day 100 !!!!
> I love you, you have been such a light in my life. . . .

This e-mail came from a married adult daughter, the same teenage girl who, years earlier, had stood in the door to the sunroom of our home in emotional darkness screaming in disbelief, with tears flooding her flushed face. With tears in my eyes as I write these words, let me tell you with absolute assurance that there is a God who loves us, a God who turns the page. He has made Himself known to us.

Several weeks later, Chris and Staci were participating in a young adult class, and the topic of regular Bible study came up. Staci, in silence, listened. Chris spoke up and shared Staci's journey. Somewhat fascinated by Staci's blossoming relationship with the Lord, the group peppered her with questions, seeking to understand. The following Sunday morning, a woman who had participated in the class approached Staci and told her, "This is Day One for me."

These are but a few of many personal experiences, and I am now absolutely certain of one thing. Bruce Wilkinson was right about miraculous multiplication. Walking in the presence of God, abiding with Him, has a multiplying effect, and you realize it has nothing to

do with you. Removing self and becoming transparent gives God the
opportunity to speak.

Fall, my favorite season, was upon us. The brightly colored leaves,
so vivid in the midday sun, were beginning to seesaw to the floor of
the forest as the gentle breeze whispered. Georgia Tech's "Ramblin'
Wreck" would soon be pouring onto Grant Field in Atlanta to open
the college football season, and I would be spending countless mornings on a deer stand in the middle Georgia woods inhaling the
presence of God with the first hint of daylight. Though I had made
that "opening day" trip every year since I was thirteen, this year
would be special, unlike any other. Never had I seen the sun lift itself
above the horizon with such a deep awareness and understanding of
God's creation.

November twenty-fifth neared. A year in God's Word, in God's
presence . . . the impossible, was now upon me. Up at 4:50 A.M.,
at the coffee shop at 5:30 A.M., with pen in hand, I wrote,
"November 25th, 2002 (Day # 365) . . ." The journey, now a part
of me, had changed my life. I went home at mid-morning and sat
down at the computer. There was a card leaning against the
computer screen. I opened it and read:

> You were my early love,
> new as a day breaking in spring.
> You were the image of everything
> that caused me to sing.

> I loved you then.
> I love you now . . .
> I will love you forever.

Congratulations . . . One year,
I am moved by your dedication
and deeply touched by the growth that is reaped.

Yours,
Jeannie

I took six steps to the door of the study where Jeannie was sitting at the desk, her back facing the morning sun. I thanked her for the card. She smiled and spoke openly and honestly. She told me that she had believed the "Read the Bible" adventure would simply be a fad, and disappear over time. She had assumed it would last a few weeks, a couple of months at the most. Though not spoken, I knew that she had begun protecting her soul from me years ago. Now she was trying, with great fear, to expose her heart. We had not escaped from the horrendous, crippling grasp of the painful memories. In fact, "we" would *never* be able to. But the Spirit of God, the master of love and forgiveness, was living in our house, and though we had no idea, we were only weeks away from experiencing His grace. It would be a spiritual struggle, but it would be God's gift of freedom.

The holidays were upon us. Megan and Jeannie were preparing to go on the church mission trip to Amsterdam, and I was teaching *Secrets of the Vine* again . . . with a new song in my heart. The Christmas season was refreshing, embodying a spirit of love and peace that our family had not experienced in years. We stayed home and relaxed, not making the customary mad dash to Macon, Georgia, on Christmas morning. We reflected, as we do every year, on the only other Christmas that we stayed home; when we spent Christmas at Children's Hospital in Dallas, Texas, with Dana, then

two years old, stricken with viral encephalitis. There is a note of
irony. On both occasions, we would see God reach into the valley of
the shadow of death, display His miraculous hand, and give life.

The day after Christmas, the family scattered like a covey of
quail. Amber and I were the only ones in Nashville. Every morning
in my time with the Lord I journaled and prayed, asking the Lord to
give Megan and Jeannie a joyous trip and safety . . . most of all, I
prayed that the Lord would touch Jeannie's heart, to reveal Himself
to her. I wrote these words, again and again.

With family dispersed throughout the United States and Europe
until the first week in January, the end of the year came quietly and
peacefully. I recorded Day Four Hundred in the Lord without event,
my spiritual journey now effortless. The New Year began and we
settled back into our routine. January would eventually prove to be
anything but routine. We would experience the impossible, the
miraculous, and it would begin on a cold, quiet winter morning.
God would speak in virtual silence.

As Elihu said in the book of Job, "God does speak— now one
way, now another . . ." (33:14). Now he would speak to us . . . in
silence. God has a reputation for making Himself known in a still
small voice. In the nineteenth chapter of 1 Kings, Elijah, a prophet
and great man of God, had grown weary and he was distraught. He
told the Lord that he'd had enough, and asked God to take his life.
The almighty God, seeing his desperation, said to him, "Go out and
stand on the mountain in the presence of the Lord, for the Lord is
about to pass by." He would speak to Elijah; uplift him with "a
gentle whisper" (vv. 11–12). The Lord would reveal Himself to us in
that same small voice and give me ears to hear. God, who had
moved into our home several months earlier, would now speak.

I came home from the coffee shop one January morning, standard routine. I walked into the game room to speak to Jeannie before going to run a few errands. She was standing at the pool table, folding clothes. I stood in the doorway to the kitchen, ten or twelve feet from her. The blinds were partially closed and the lights were off, the room softly lit with the early morning sun. Our conversation was brief and insignificant. I have no recollection of what we talked about. I turned, walked through the kitchen, and started down the stairs to the basement . . . and I knew. The certainty of the truth was not evident in the words she spoke, neither in her facial expression, nor the inflection in her voice. The "gentle whisper" which had become so familiar to me was clear. I knew. The invisible wind of change that had engulfed my heart was blowing again . . . in Jeannie's soul. The impossible was happening.

I retraced my steps into the house in the late afternoon. I opened the door to the kitchen and saw Jeannie preparing dinner. She had her back to me. My first words to her, verbatim, were, "Something is happening to you." She wheeled around, and with a somewhat dismissive tone said, "What are you talking about?" I said, "Something is happening to you," as I patted my heart with my right hand. Jeannie, teary-eyed, said, "I have fought this [the Lord] as long as I can." She turned away.

Quietly, gracefully, without fanfare, she was spending time in God's Word. Two, three, four days passed. For years, Jeannie had stepped gingerly in my presence, every word chosen with caution, armor in place, the soul protected. On a warm, sunny winter morning, with the sun shining brightly onto her open Bible, she placed her reading glasses on the table and said, "I have placed myself and our children entirely under your spiritual leadership . . .

because I see that you have totally committed yourself to the Lord."
Then, in a moment that we shall both remember for a lifetime, she
looked at me, smiled, and said, "And if you haven't, we are both
screwed." The levity of the moment was priceless. For the first time
in years, longer than either of us could remember, we drank from the
same cup at God's fountain.

In the days that followed, we would simply sit and talk . . . and
smile. I looked into the face of the mother of our five children, and
I saw the peaceful teenage girl that I married. It had been a long
time. She was no longer a prisoner. The living God opened the door,
and she walked into my arms.

For the prior fourteen months, more than four hundred days, I
had been on a journey. On God's spiritual highway, I had gained
momentum and made significant progress, but my experience, while
rewarding, had been incomplete. Now, with the January sun setting,
our Creator blanketed Nashville with a beautiful snowfall. The glis-
tening midnight moon shone brightly, the snow-covered ground
reflecting the brilliance of a new day, Day One of "our" journey.
After a long journey in darkness, we caught a glimmer of hope and
grasped the presence of the living God together, and understood
who God was—who God *really* was.

We had battled desperately, for years, working independently of
each other and of God to resolve our problems. Suddenly, we were
standing together, trusting not in each other, but in the living God.
The significance of this moment cannot be found in man's apology
and forgiveness, but in trusting the Lord. There is no other way. Such
forgiveness, such healing of the soul, is beyond the human mind; it is
found in the heart of God, a love that "keeps no record of wrongs"
(1 Cor. 13:5). This spiritual truth is deeply embedded in our story.

The heart of God reaches beyond the powerful grasp of life's difficult circumstances, beyond paralyzing pain, and beyond our basic human nature. God's love and mercy transform the heart, giving hope where there is no hope. This great spiritual truth is God's painful gift, the promise of "hope as an anchor for the soul, firm and secure" (Heb. 6:19).

Jeannie and I live and speak with a spirit of faith, because we live in His presence. For a very long and painful season of life, our family suffered terribly, every soul harmed beyond description. We were wasting away, one heartbeat at a time. With the presence of God's miraculous loving hand, we did not lose heart, and now, day-by-day, He is renewing us. Our lives will not be free of momentary troubles, but the painful gifts that God has given us will outweigh them all. We no longer focus on that which is seen in our midst. We, like Moses, the great man of faith, now look to that which is unseen, the very presence of God. Our daily challenges and dilemmas are temporary, but our hope is eternal. So was Paul's message to the church at Corinth in the fourth chapter of 2 Corinthians, and so it is to us.

The spiraling cycle of human nature had been our life. For years, life's paralyzing pain had devastated us. Circumstances controlled our existence, and we fought desperately for survival. Then, God did what no other could do. He reached into the life of the lone ranger, a mere shell of a man, and lifted me up, breaking the cycle in our lives.

The joy of this moment is somewhat overwhelming. The mountaintop, God's spiritual pinnacle, is glorious. We want to simply stop and rest right here and savor the moment. But my mind intervenes with the realization that emotional mountaintops burn off like the early morning fog. The sizzling sensation of the love story will give way to the harsh reality of life when we face tomorrow's sunrise. Thus, I am compelled to paint this joyful picture in a structured approach that will give you a practical roadmap leading to the powerful presence of the living God.

Chapter nine, "The Promise of Hope," will portray that power; giving life to a personal journey in which our relationship with God is our primary focus. I will present the Spiritual Cycle, the opportunity that each of us has to break away from our basic crippling human nature and experience the living God, to see hope on the horizon. Living in God's presence, the mystery of abiding is at our fingertips.

CHAPTER NINE

The Promise of Hope

"This is what the Lord says:
'. . . blessed is the man who trusts in the Lord,
whose confidence is in him.
He will be like a tree planted by the water
that sends out its roots by the stream.
It does not fear when heat comes;
its leaves are always green.
It has no worries in a year of drought
and never fails to bear fruit.'"
—Jeremiah 17:5, 7–8

The Great Escape

As we seek God's promise of hope in the Spiritual Cycle, let's be certain that we are grounded in the truth. In chapter four, "Human Nature," we journeyed deep into our basic human nature and took a truthful look at our everyday lives. We faced the harsh reality that we habitually relegate God to a subordinate position and empower the circumstances of life to control our thinking, our decision making, and our behavior.

When faced with life's difficult circumstances, we naturally muster our personal willpower and determination, and we attack, pursuing our "own course like a horse charging into battle" (Jer. 8:6). We fight our battles alone. We rejoice when the giant has been slain . . . when the sin monger is dead, when life's painful circumstances are behind us. We declare victory.

Naïvely, we have come to view painful circumstances as the author of darkness. We embrace calm waters as the joyful conclusion, the picture of success. Nothing could be further from the truth.

> *The crippling, paralyzing impact*
> *of difficult circumstances is not "the problem,"*
> *it is the "the symptom" . . . of an absentee God.*

> *Calm waters are not "the solution,"*
> *they are a "band-aid" . . . a short-lived substitution*
> *for embracing the heart of God.*

As we go it alone and distance ourselves from the heart of God, He withholds His thoughts and His guidance (Prov. 1:23–27). Alone we labor, day after day, tackling one problem after another. We are lifted to the crest of one wave of life only to be swamped by the next breaker. Calamity overtakes us. Blind-sided and disoriented, we rarely extend a hand in God's direction until we are going under for the third and final time.

As we experienced together in chapter four, the result of God's absence is most often a downward emotional spiral, a condition I termed cyclical misery. The Human Cycle is an emotionally depleting journey from which we seemingly cannot escape. As we concluded earlier, we are basically addicted to the self-will. If we are honest, willing to momentarily put our carefully polished spiritual shells aside and look within our souls, we find the truth deep within the Human Cycle. We simply need a mirror. We have found the enemy—and it is us. The decisions we make are of our own choosing. God gives us the freedom to go it alone. We have opted to embrace life's circumstances as our internal compass and guide.

We now face the challenge of breaking the choking grip of the Human Cycle. The opportunity we have to enter into God's presence, as portrayed in the Spiritual Cycle, is easy to grasp intellectually, but it requires more than understanding. It demands a change of heart. The escape from the Human Cycle, the first step toward God's promise of hope, embodies the very essence of Neil Armstrong's first words, "One small step for man, one giant leap for mankind," as he stepped onto the moon. Catching the vision of the Spiritual Cycle is one small step of understanding, but one giant leap for the heart. It is a true break from our regimented spiritual heritage into God's realm, an unknown world for many of us. The first small step has giant implications. It is a step of faith, a step that reaches beyond the mind, beyond the intellect, and into the heart.

For many of us, the Spiritual Cycle is a journey into uncharted waters. We hesitate because the very concept of God's living presence and His consistent influence in our daily lives is foreign to us. It makes us uneasy. Truthfully, we have a much greater comfort level living in the Human Cycle, where we have control. Even with its inherent struggles, we prefer it.

We should not be surprised. Maintaining control is basically what we have been taught and have experienced for a lifetime. We have embraced this human dilemma for years and we have adapted to the emotional struggle, learning to manage and survive. We did not become the lone ranger overnight. We learned one day at a time.

The journey into the living presence of God, the Spiritual Cycle, is no different. It is not instantaneous. It is not magical, not your

basic rabbit-in-a-hat trick. It is a journey, a committed journey of
long-suffering, seeking, and rejoicing.

The Spiritual Cycle, like the Human Cycle, visually depicts our
thought processes and our basic decision-making style. The basic
format of the Spiritual Cycle displays "circumstances" and our
"relationship with God" as the two primary factors that construct
our thinking. Again, for ease of explanation, circumstances are
defined as being either "good" or "bad"; and our relationship with
God as either "weak" or "strong." This approach, while simplistic,
effectively communicates the message.

As we make the transition to the Spiritual Cycle, you may be
surprised at its striking similarity to the Human Cycle. Most
notably, though God grows to be preeminent in our lives, difficult
circumstances in life are ever-present. No matter how glorious our
walk with the Lord becomes, life continues to be tough. Yes, bad
things do happen to good people. But as we will see, life's challenges take on new meaning when our relationship with God
changes.

The most profound difference found in the Spiritual Cycle is the
strength we discover by dwelling in God's presence. In so doing, we
relegate the circumstances of life to a secondary role, no longer
allowing them to control our thinking, our decision making, and our
emotional stability.

As we will discover in the Spiritual Cycle, the journey into the
heart of God requires personal commitment. It is not a cakewalk.
Figure 7, the Spiritual Cycle, identical to figure 6 in the Human
Cycle, summarizes the repetitive struggle of the lone ranger. As you
will recall from our detailed review in chapter four, this diagram
reflects our go-it-alone strategy of the "self will" that results in life's

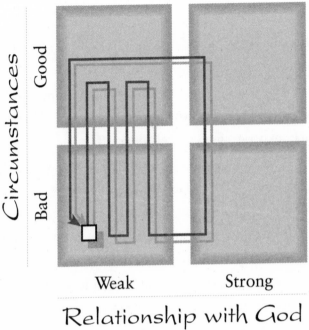

Fig. 7.

circumstance-driven emotional roller coaster. We muster our personal will and determination again and again, only to wallow in frustration and, ultimately, desperation.

We know with certainty that we are not alone in our struggle. As we see in the fifty-seventh chapter of Isaiah, our spiritual heritage clearly indicates that cyclical misery is in our spiritual gene pool. As the Lord speaks to the prophet Isaiah, His words appear to have been written for us:

> You were wearied by all your ways,
> but you would not say, "It is hopeless."
> You found renewal of your strength,
> and so you did not faint (v. 10).

The Israelites were tired, "wearied" by their lone-ranger strategy, but they did not seek God's guidance. They, like us, depended on their strength and forged ahead.

Yet, despite having such great biblical insight and warning at our fingertips, our basic nature is to put God on the sidelines and neglect His guidance. This is the very behavior that keeps us on life's humanistic racetrack, experiencing cyclical misery. This is a tragic pattern that we must break if we are to experience God's gift of hope.

In chapter three, "The Lone Ranger," I purposely shared my personal story, embodied in the shell-shocked silence of the poem "Overload." It is my deepest desire that you hear my heartbeat exploding in my eardrums, that you see the faces of little girls who are lost without their daddy, and that you suffer with my teenage bride as her dreams are shattered right before her eyes. For it is in the explosiveness of devastation that God's powerful hand is often made known. We find Him in the midst of the struggle. In the valley of the shadow of death, we need not fear, for He is with us. In our weakness, He seemingly emerges from the darkness bearing the gift of hope.

The Heart of God

"He tends his flock like a shepherd:
He gathers the lambs in his arms
and carries them close to his heart;
he gently leads those who have young."
—Isaiah 40:11

We surrender, perhaps for the first time in our lives. We truly surrender self. We lay down all our cards and quit negotiating with

God. We put our eleventh-hour deal-making aside. We no longer call on God for an emergency rescue attempt. We search for God's heart. We seek His path (see fig. 8).

Let's step into God's presence and listen as He speaks. The Bible provides us a glimpse of the missing link in the Forty-Sixth Psalm:

> God is our refuge and strength,
>
> an ever-present help in trouble.
>
> Therefore we will not fear,
>
> though the earth give way
>
> and the mountains fall into the heart of the sea . . . (vv. 1–2).

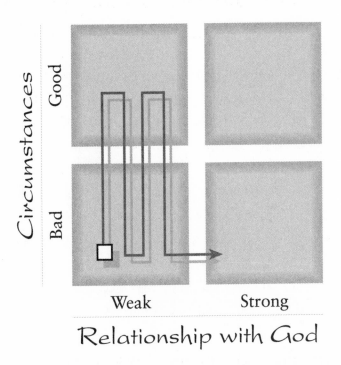

Relationship with God

Fig. 8.

The essence of the Spiritual Cycle is embedded in this passage. Living a life of independence, we have failed to embrace God as our source of "refuge and strength, an ever-present help" when the "earth [was giving] way." We have missed it. We have failed to see God as the author of hope, an anchor for the soul.

We need to know why.

If we are to experience God, alive in the Spiritual Cycle, it is a question that must be answered.

The only question that Debbie asked me is before us again. It remains unanswered. "Why . . . why in the midst of a living hell, life's paralyzing pain, can I find no understanding, no guidance, no peace . . . no hope? As the earth gives way, why is God of no help to me?"

In chapter two, "Living in Innocence," I asked the question, but intentionally gave little as an answer. I identified the major dilemma we face, the problem of spiritual *unawareness*, spiritual sharecropping:

> Sadly . . . our Christianity, our personal walk with God, is defined primarily by our relationships with Christian friends and our involvement in church activities. The person of God is nowhere to be found.

And I drew a sound intellectual conclusion:

> We, like Job, need to grow to see God as "Who we serve," not just "Why we serve."

In the midst of fact-finding and spiritual investigation, I identified the Church as the epicenter of our Christian walk and deemed us to be lacking in the depth of our personal relationship with God. Our spiritual leaders have shared this truth time and time again. Though these words ring true to our ears, they are relatively meaningless to us. Intellectually, we find them to be true, but they lack impact. They do not give us hope.

The question remains with us—"Why . . . why in the midst of a living hell, life's paralyzing pain, can we not find understanding, guidance, peace . . . hope?" It remains unanswered in our hearts.

I turn to Philip Yancey's book *What's So Amazing About Grace*, and the hidden truth begins to emerge. He quotes Thomas Merton with a simple, powerful insight:

We cannot find Him unless we know we need Him.

Pain, the harsh reality of paralyzing pain, is not in question, it is a universal language. The fact that we desperately need help is undeniable. *We know* that we need help. We search for help. We search everywhere . . . everywhere that we know to look. We walk the aisles of the self-help section of the bookstore, scanning the titles for insight into our personal struggles. The shelves are filled. Everything is there, from A to Z, anorexia to Zen. Our insatiable demand for help has created a multimillion-dollar psychotherapy industry. Our churches have invested in staff members devoted to spiritual counseling. We leave no stone unturned in our desperate search. There is no question about the certainty of pain.

I value the contribution found in modern self-help literature, and I believe that God has ordained men and women to provide immeasurable assistance in the midst of crisis. But as we look closely, there is something missing . . . something extraordinarily important.

Thomas Merton's quote, "We cannot find Him unless we know we need Him," does not question the need for help. He questions whether or not we see the living God as being of any value in our struggle. Our day-to-day behavior speaks. We do not believe we "need Him." The Human Cycle, presented in chapter four, displays this truth vividly. We tend to seek God's guidance only as a last resort, seriously doubting He will be of any help, and we quietly drift away from Him when our circumstances improve. We talk church. The old adage, "Actions speak louder than words," is alive and well. We seek help; but we do not seek it from the person of God. We must confront the truth. We simply do not believe "we need *Him*." Like our spiritual ancestors, we assume our troubles are hidden from God. We believe He has disregarded us. We are in good company . . . that is precisely what the Israelites thought (Isa. 40:27).

So now, we must answer this question . . . "Why?"
Why do we not know that "we need Him"?

Do not miss this moment. Slightly camouflaged, hidden from our view, this was Debbie's question. When I felt as if I had come to the "tragic end," it was also my question. When Tracie wrote of fear, it was her question. When you face life's tragedies and struggle in darkness without hope, it is your question. It is a question that we must not leave unanswered. We must determine why we do not consistently seek the heart of God. It is time to step out of the lunar landing module with Neil Armstrong. The answer is a small step of intellectual understanding . . . and a giant leap in the transformation of the heart. It is the key to hope in the midst of paralyzing pain.

Reflecting upon Merton's quote, Philip Yancey comments that for someone raised in a strong church background, that awareness of needing God might not come easily. Those of us deeply ingrained in the church have a tendency to not know that "we need Him." Our daily spiritual walk excludes the person of God. What incredible irony . . . the cobbler's children have no shoes! Yancey's words scream a silent, virtually invisible truth. Many of us reared in the church have never experienced God's magnificent power, His miraculous hand. I had not; I had never really needed His help. He had never rescued me when I was going under for the third and final time. I knew about desperation, "utter lack of hope," only through Webster's dictionary. I had never groped in darkness and experienced the powerful principle of "radical dependence on a higher power" embraced and espoused by Alcoholics Anonymous. God was commonplace to me, a relatively insignificant fixture in my mind.

My journey, my simplistic spiritual grasp of "who God was," frighteningly mirrors the hearts of many and penetrates the entire body of spiritual believers. No one is immune. No one. The spiritual newness has long since worn off.

> *For those of us deeply ingrained in the church,*
> *living a life of knowing "we need Him"*
> *does not come easily.*

"Why do we need Him?" is often a difficult question for us to answer. With frightening regularity, God rests as a fixture in our minds. He is stationary. He is a mere object in our spiritual world. Patrick Morley, in the book *Second Wind for the Second Half*, paints this picture in living color:

> God talk runs high; God walk runs low. Why is that? As a culture we speak highly of God, but often as an enfeebled grandfather, appreciated for what he did in times past. It's not that we don't think highly of God—we do. We just don't think of him as relevant.

As was the case with Job, He is "why we serve," not "who we serve." We turn our back on this truth. Such a perspective of God is simply unheard of and unacceptable inside the walls of the church. Far too often, it is what we believe in our hearts, but we cannot speak it.

Why do "we need Him?"
Our answer is . . . we believe we don't.

Our daily actions confirm this unspeakable truth. It is time we face it.

We meditate on the Forty-Sixth Psalm, and we easily grasp the reality of the "earth [giving] way." It equates to our modern-day challenges, which we have come to experience painfully. Our "needing Him" to assist us, to help us in our daily struggles, is much more vague and difficult to believe. The spiritual answer to "Why . . . why in the midst of a living hell, life's paralyzing pain, can I find no understanding, no guidance, no peace . . . no hope?" is embedded in the Forty-Sixth Psalm:

God is our refuge and strength,

an ever-present help in trouble.

Therefore, we will not fear . . . (vv. 1–2).

God, as an intellectual Savior, a part-time participant neatly woven into our lives, an "enfeebled grandfather," is not a source of "refuge and strength, an ever-present help." God, carefully compartmentalized in our lives, does not give us hope. He is not an anchor for the soul. He does not give us a sense of security in troubled times.

We read these words—refuge, strength, and ever-present—and they sound so "Old Testament," just Bible-talk. We have a tendency to dismiss them as irrelevant to modern times and just move on to the New Testament where Jesus Himself showed up. Perhaps we should look to Webster for understanding:

Refuge	*n.* shelter or protection.
Strength	*n.* force, power, vigor.
Ever	*adv.* always, at any time.
Present	*adj.* being at hand.

In simpler terminology, the first verse of the Forty-Sixth Psalm comes to life:

God is our source of power and protection
all the time.

"All the time" has life-changing implications. The very concept destroys our view of God as intellectual in nature, part-time, and compartmentalized. "All the time" enters the spiritual world of indwelling and abiding with God—it speaks loudly of a meaningful personal relationship. For those of us deeply entrenched on our religious paths, such a thought is . . . honestly . . . well, unfamiliar and uncomfortable. It does not fit our spiritual mold of living independently. This paints a picture unlike the God we know.

We tend to view a spiritual relationship with God in the strictest sense—off or on, the ultimate picture of clarity. It is the sheep and the goats, heaven or hell. Once we are "in," hell is in our rear-view mirror. We have joined the sheep . . . case closed.

Many of us have missed it. The answer to "Why . . . why in the midst of a living hell, life's paralyzing pain, can I find no understanding, no guidance, no peace . . . no hope?" is not found in simply "believing" in God. The answer . . . hope . . . is found in walking in His path, seeking His guidance, and trusting His heart . . . all the time.

As I came to this place in the text, this critical moment of giving life to the invisible . . . the certainty of hope . . . found in a heart-felt relationship with God, I found myself searching for words to convey God's heart. In our pastor's absence, Mack Hannah, the vice president of spiritual affairs at Belmont University, stood before the Sunday morning congregation and posed this simple but thought-provoking question:

"When did you become a follower of Christ?"

He paused, drifted quietly across the platform, and left the congregation to ponder the moment. Silence was golden. As he lifted his face and prepared to speak, the camera zoomed in, his face magnified on two large screens in the sanctuary. Softly, gently, in his own mild-mannered style, he threw a spiritual grenade into the conservative crowd. He said, "I did not ask when you became a believer. I am not asking when you made a personal profession of faith. My question is, 'When did you become a follower?'"

His question rocks our spiritual world. His question explodes the "sheep and goat" theory. Our journey of breaking the Human Cycle and embracing the heart of God in the Spiritual Cycle is not a simple question of heaven or hell. It is not a light switch. We are not "off or on." In a bit of irony, his question exposes the obvious. In the text of His message, the fourth chapter of Matthew, Jesus challenges His disciples with these straight-forward words, "Come, follow me." They speak to the heart of our personal struggle in the midst of pain; relinquish control, seek God's face . . . and follow.

Mack Hannah shared the truth about being a follower. First and foremost, we, like the disciples, are called to follow. Being a follower has far-reaching spiritual implications. It means:

1. There is a leader . . . and I am not him.
2. There is a way . . . and I do not know it.

It means there is a leader who knows the way, and I must learn to trust His judgment. It means I must follow. It means there is no place for the lone ranger in God's message, in God's heart.

Being a follower *is not about convenience, comfort, or conditions.* It is not about seeking God's guidance or honoring his direction "if, if, if. . . . " In the spirit of the Human Cycle, it is not about circumstances. Being a follower is not about living on life's emotional roller coaster. Being a follower *is about calling, communication, and commitment.* It is about our relationship with God being a priority. If we are to experience His grace, *following* is not optional.

Mack's conclusion, elementary as it was, brought a smile to my face. He said, "Followers . . . well, they follow." They do not allow the circumstances of life to derail their walk with God. The answer to "Why . . . why in the midst of a living hell, life's paralyzing pain, can I find no understanding, no guidance, no peace . . . no hope?" is found in *following* . . . walking in His path, seeking His guidance, and trusting His heart . . . all the time.

Following requires denying self by putting life's circumstances and personal willpower aside and "[taking] up his cross daily" (Luke 9:23). Jesus guides us to embrace Him as our source of power and protection. "Daily," the picture of consistency, is the key ingredient. It is the magic. It is the heartbeat of knowing the living God and finding hope.

This message brings such clarity to our struggle. "Following Him," embracing the heart of God as a source of power and protection all the time, not only answers the question of "Why?"; it also provides insight into the freeing gift of breaking out of the Human Cycle and personally experiencing God in the Spiritual Cycle, the pure joy of living in His presence. This is the essence of our spiritual journey together.

I could end the book right here . . . but we would likely fail to grasp the heart of God as our promise of hope. Knowing about God is one thing—seeing the invisible is an entirely different experience.

With experience as our teacher, we know that seeing, believing, and following the invisible God is not easy. We want to break out, but we find ourselves struggling. We intellectually believe the truth of the living God, but at times we hesitate, and it all seems somewhat mythical, distant . . . just spiritual stuff.

I know the feeling. In my time in the morning in God's Word, I felt Him. I personally experienced God's growing presence. In undeniable fashion, He came alive in Scripture. He moved visibly within our home. Yet, in the midst of my personal journey, it was not uncommon for me to search the starry sky in the blackness of the night and ask: "Really?", "When?", and "How?" Then, that which I knew to be true, that which I had experienced in my heart and mind, was revealed to me in the flesh.

In my months of sharing time with the Lord at the coffee shop, I have met and spent time with many men and women. There have been a number of interesting relationships that have been characterized by a "knowing nod." These were the men and women who simply *knew*. On a daily basis, they observed my commitment to God's Word, and they nodded with a quiet, supportive gesture. Nowhere was this more evident than in the face of a middle-aged man who caught my eye and nodded his head graciously, with the slightest hint of a smile, almost indistinguishable. He entered and exited, most often unnoticed, but his virtual silence did nothing to camouflage the presence of God in his eyes. I knew with certainty he was a man of God, and I knew he was deep.

He drove a white van with a metal rack and ladders on top. His transportation and casual business appearance led me to conclude that he was involved in construction. He was always in and out quickly, a man with a lot to get done. He was there almost every day. Saturdays were unique; he and a friend would sit and play chess for an hour or so, with the same aura of silence that characterized his weekday visits. Quietly in, chess, quietly out . . . month after month. He and I had never spoken, until one divine morning.

I was alone at my table, and he was preparing his coffee. I turned and spoke to him. He walked around the cream and sugar bar and sat down in front of me. Our initial conversation was casual, his foreign accent strong. Acknowledging the obvious, I asked where he was from. He said, "Russia." My heart flooded. For the next hour, he sat patiently, so very gracious, while I turned into a battering ram of questions . . . one after another after another. He answered every question with his habitual quiet tone, humility displayed in every word.

Genady, born in the Soviet Union during the height of communism and the Cold War, grew up in a Christian family. His personal experience with the Lord, caught in the explosive crossfire of religion and communism, was unbelievable—church services at 3 A.M. in the woods to avoid the KGB; being arrested by the KGB, interrogated at headquarters, and told at gunpoint to denounce Christ or be shot; being forced to work as a laborer because he was a Christian despite his college degrees in engineering and economics; and ultimately leaving Russia for the United States (Russia to Austria to Italy to New York) with his wife and five children (ages two through twelve), seven suitcases, the clothes on their backs, and one thousand dollars. When his family landed in New York City, his total grasp of the English language was, "My name is Genady."

I was overwhelmed. As Elihu says in the book of Job, "God does speak—now one way, now another." That Friday morning was an incredible spiritual experience for me. God Himself, in the body of His servant and witness Genady Prutianov, revealed the true meaning of following, surrender of self. More than once Genady had refused to denounce Christ, fully anticipating a bullet in his temple. He was willing to die for God. He had walked in the fiery furnace with Shadrach, Meshach, and Abednego. Genady had:

> Trusted in him and defied the [KGB's] command and [was] willing to give up [his life] rather than serve or worship any god except [his] own God (Dan. 3:28).

For me, it was the true picture, in perfect focus. Genady knew the answer to "Why?" He had looked down the barrel of a gun and lived it. He had faced life's paralyzing pain and found hope, an anchor for his soul. God lived in his heart. In the midst of life's tragic circumstances, God was Genady's source of power and protection all the time. He knew what it meant to be a follower; he was one.

Our question:

> *Why . . . why in the midst of a living hell,*
> *life's paralyzing pain,*
> *can I find no understanding, no guidance,*
> *no peace . . . no hope?*

has an answer. Be a follower, seek the face of the living God, grow into His presence, and know that:

> *God is our source of power and protection*
> *all the time.*

This message is sprinkled throughout the Bible. It touches kings, prophets, and yes, the woman at the well. God's message is for everyone, all the time. God Himself speaks these beautiful words to the prophet Isaiah. They were God's gift to comfort His chosen people in their time of trouble. They ring true in our time. Let us have ears to hear and a heart to see.

> Do you not know?
> Have you not heard?
> The Lord is the everlasting God,
> the Creator of the ends of the earth.
> He will not grow tired or weary,
> and his understanding no one can fathom.
> He gives strength to the weary
> and increases the power of the weak.
> Even youths grow tired and weary,
> and young men stumble and fall;
> but those who hope in the Lord
> will renew their strength.
> They will soar on wings like eagles;
> they will run and not grow weary,
> they will walk and not be faint (Isa. 40:28–31).

We know. We have heard. In the face of life's paralyzing difficult circumstances, God, our Creator, is always present, giving strength when we stumble and fall. He will renew our strength, and we will soar on wings like eagles. God is our source of power and protection all the time. This truth is the heart of the Spiritual Cycle.

In God's Word, we have discovered the power that releases us from the misery, the crippling devastation of the Human Cycle. We have grasped the heartfelt spiritual reality, the truth of who God is.

We no longer face circumstantial paralysis. We are no longer alone.
As we grow to seek God's face, we have His power and protection
available to us all the time.

Building the Wall

"I looked for a man among them
who would build up the wall
and stand before me in the gap
on behalf of the land. . . ."
—Ezekiel 22:30

The concept of abiding in Christ, the mystery that we first
addressed in chapter six, is within reach. God's presence begins to
overflow in our hearts. This newfound, spiritually enriching journey
comes to life. We are on the right path, His path. Our stoic picture
of God crumbles, giving way to an image of a living God who sees
our misery, hears our cries, is concerned about our suffering, and is
coming to rescue us (Exod. 3:8). It is the dawning of a new day in
our hearts.

Let caution be our guide as we embark. This journey of pure
spiritual joy is not a euphoric weekend youth retreat. You know
exactly what I mean—spiritually inspired on Friday night, tearful
jubilation by Saturday evening, and a distant memory two weeks
later. No, our journey is not an instantaneous celebratory mountaintop experience. It is a marathon . . . a joyful struggle of
long-suffering, seeking, and rejoicing.

Previously a mere instrument manipulated by life's circumstances, an arrow in Satan's quiver, we now emerge as spiritual
warriors . . . a viable spiritual threat. The presence of God is

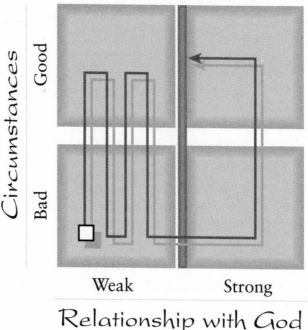

Fig. 9.

growing in our hearts and characters. The power of life's circumstances in our lives gives way to God's influence. The very presence of evil in our midst is challenged and weakened. People look into our eyes and see the emerging face of God. This reality is a great biblical truth. The abiding presence of the Lord is undeniable.

The spiritual battle for our very souls is underway. The magnetic pull of the independent self is ever-present, lurking in the shadows, seeking to destroy. As we grow to experience the power of God in the Spiritual Cycle, we remain constantly at risk of losing our spiritual focus as life's painful circumstantial grip releases us, as darkness gives way to light. We have been here before and failed to hold on to the hand of God. We understand the power of *invisible risk*, and it is a tremendous threat. We know how difficult it is to walk consistently in His path. We have experienced it. This is spiritual warfare.

We have seen the heart of God; our eyes have been opened. It is hand-to-hand combat. It is time to go on the offensive, time to protect ourselves from life's destructive forces, the crippling emotional roller coaster of circumstances and the powerful force of self-interest. It is time for us to build a protective spiritual wall (see fig. 9).

The destructive forces and inherent dangers in life are formidable. If we are to be successful in protecting our hearts and souls, we must be committed to flawless blueprints and quality construction. We must know:

1. *Why* we will build—a commitment to a higher purpose,
2. *What* we will build with—spiritually grounded planning principles, and
3. *How* we will build—a consistent process.

It is essential that we be committed to the purpose, the planning principles, and the process.

The Purpose

The wall is the foundation of transforming the heart. This lifelong building process gives life to our spiritual renewal and provides protection from circumstantial misery. Our purpose is crystallized in our hearts. We build to ensure that we are grounded in His Word, walk consistently in His path, are protected by His hand, and grow to be living instruments for His purpose.

We build the wall to defend ourselves. We guard ourselves from those outside forces that "so easily entangle" us (Heb. 12:1).

We build to protect ourselves from the very presence of evil. We build, "in order that Satan might not outwit us. For we are not unaware of his schemes" (2 Cor. 2:11). We have experienced the overpowering force of self, the very absence of God. We have carried the flag of the lone ranger and have been embroiled in the circumstances of life. We build in order that God's constant presence, His magnificent power, might overcome the daily onslaught that life sends our way. We build to defend, to protect our hearts.

We build the wall to grow spiritually. The wall rises from a stable foundation and reaches skyward, one stone at a time. Stone by stone, day by day, the wall grows in size and strength. God's Word gives light where there is darkness. As we grow in God's presence, we grow in our spiritual stature. Our expanding knowledge of God's Word gives us insight into the heart of God, His character, and His purpose. We are building a wall of spiritual strength . . . a wall that cannot be penetrated. We are not alone. We, like Moses, grow to see "the invisible God" in our daily walk. We no longer face spiritual sharecropping. We walk with Him. We build the wall for personal spiritual renewal.

We build the wall in order that our lives might reflect His love. We build to transform the inner heart so that we will outwardly reflect the character of God. We build in order that we become living instruments for His purpose. We build that we might share His love. Jesus, in the flesh, gave us blueprints for the wall, "Love each other as I have loved you" (John 15:12). As Dallas Willard so beautifully portrays in *Renovation of the Heart*:

> It is love itself, not loving behavior, or even the wish or intent to love—that has the power to always protect, always trust, always

hope, put up with anything, and never quit (1 Cor. 13:7–8). Merely trying to act lovingly will lead to despair and to the defeat of love. It will make us angry and hopeless. But taking love itself—God's kind of love—into the depths of our being through spiritual formation will, by contrast, enable us to act lovingly to an extent that will be surprising even to ourselves, at first. And this love will then become a constant source of joy and refreshment to ourselves and others.

We build to reflect the heart of God. We build so that His character is consistently revealed in our lives; "so that we can comfort those in any trouble with the comfort we ourselves have received from God" (2 Cor. 1:4). We build so that we might be a light to the world, a city on the hill (Matt. 5:14).

As our spiritual wall grows day by day, our relationship with God grows strong and consistent. We walk in His path, and our everyday lives grow to reflect His heart and character. Our hearts extend beyond loving behavior, beyond good works. Those in our midst look into our eyes and at our actions, and they see beyond us; they see God's presence emerging in our transformed hearts. They see the love of God revealed in our lives. They see spiritual fruitfulness.

And God is able to make all grace abound to you, so that in all things at all times, having all that you need, you will abound in every good work (2 Cor. 9:8).

As we build the wall and grow spiritually, we come face-to-face with our greater purpose, God's purpose, to be bearers of spiritual fruit.

As we prepare to construct a spiritually grounded plan, we do so with the three key points of our purpose clearly in mind. We are building a wall in order that we:

1. Defend and protect our heart,
2. Grow in spirit and understanding, and
3. Become living instruments for God's greater purpose.

The Principles of Planning

Honoring His purpose does not come without devotion, without paying a price. It requires that we have spiritually grounded planning principles. Grasping the presence of God and walking consistently in His path requires personal commitment, spiritual integrity, and discipline.

In the mid-1980s, when our family lived in Atlanta, I would coordinate my drive time home from work almost every day and listen to James Dobson's radio ministry, "Focus on the Family." One afternoon, Dr. Dobson opened the half-hour program by introducing his guest and the topic of "Parenting Teenagers: Quality versus Quantity Time." Apologetically, I am unable to recall the name of his special guest that afternoon, for it was in the wisdom of this "mystery man" that we, the listeners, received a true parental gift. The gist of his message was as follows: "Parents who wave the 'quality time' banner are looking for an excuse to justify the fact that their personal priorities do not provide for 'quantity time' with their children." Then he threw the grenade over the radio waves. He said, and I paraphrase, "You cannot have quality time with your teenagers without having quantity time." He proceeded to share that quality time with them simply cannot be scheduled. He said that quality time with a teenager is a magical event that just happens. If you do not spend quantity time with your teenagers, you will miss the magical moments—the quality time.

At the time, our oldest daughter was approximately ten years old, so we had not yet experienced the mystery of teenagers. Though intrigued by his message, it did not ring true in my ears. Time would prove Dr. Dobson's guest to be a modern-day prophet. As our family grew into the teenage years, we would see the magic again and again. Out of the fog, these beautiful young people would appear for the most pleasant fifteen-minute conversation, only to disappear again with suddenness, for no apparent reason at all. If you have teenagers, you know exactly what I mean. Dr. Dobson's guest was correct. If you do not spend quantity time with your teenagers, you will miss the quality moments.

There is a corollary to his message. If you miss the quality moments, the relationship deteriorates. If the relationship deteriorates, you have given birth to the lone ranger. A teenager riding atop the horse of the lone ranger is dangerous.

My spiritual journey taught me that this insightful parenting principle has an identical application in our relationship with God. It is the commitment of quantity time, a discipline to be consistently in God's presence, that opens the floodgates and allows us to experience quality time with God. As I shared in chapter six:

> Too often . . . we plan our work, we work our plan, and we are mystified that God is not there.

We attempt to schedule quality time with God. It does not work that way. We cannot simply enter God's name in a designated slot on our calendars and expect Him to show up. Continuing the quote from chapter six:

> I am convinced that we should focus less and less on serving and obeying, and focus more and more on devoting our hearts and souls to simply seeking the Lord.

We need to simply walk in His path. In devoting our hearts and souls to seeking, we commit to quantity time with God. We walk in His path, rest in His presence, and experience quality time with Him.

As we like to say, "Half the battle is just showing up." The principle of that old adage is spiritually sound. Quantity time is a critical planning principle in building a protective spiritual wall. Remember, in the absence of quantity time, we fail to experience joyful quality time with God. In the absence of a quality spiritual journey, our relationship with God deteriorates and we are the lone ranger . . . again. Quantity time is an absolute must in spiritual wall building.

In the twenty-third verse of the ninth chapter of Luke, Jesus says, "If anyone would come after me, he must deny himself and take up his cross daily. . . ." If just showing up is half the battle, we need only look to that very same Scripture passage in Luke to complete the key spiritual planning principles. Simply, yet powerfully stated, if we are to build a protective wall to follow Him, we must take up our cross, be committed every day. Spiritual building requires that we seek.

The cornerstone of our protective wall is found in one simple word . . . seeking. If we are to abide in God's presence, rest in His protective shadow, and be an instrument for His greater purpose, *seeking* is not optional. It is an absolute, a spiritual directive. Throughout the Bible, from King David and the Mosaic Law to Jesus and the New Covenant, God directs us to seek Him. King David counseled Solomon and the Israelites to "devote [their] heart[s] and soul[s] to seeking the Lord" (1 Chron. 22:19). David had experienced the journey of the lone ranger in his lifetime and personally understood the disastrous implications.

Jesus, in the Sermon on the Mount, taught His followers to "seek first his kingdom and his righteousness" (Matt. 6:33). He guides us to stop focusing our attention primarily on life's circumstances, "worrying about tomorrow." He directs us to seek Him, to grow into His presence, to know Him. His Word gives us the promise, the assurance, that if we seek Him, we will find Him. Do not miss the power of His words. He did not first direct the New Testament Church to serve or obey. He directed them to seek Him. Jesus knew that we would grasp everything else if we searched our hearts and understood the power of His heart.

> *Devote your heart and soul to seeking,*
> *"seek first His kingdom,"*
> *"seek and you will find,"*
> *. . . seek.*

We understand it biblically, but what does this directive of "seeking" mean to us in spiritual wall building? Seek(ing)/search(ing) means to try to discover, as by studying; try to obtain; examining thoroughly; penetrating; piercing; exploring.

In a spirit of directness and blunt honesty, the heart of the definition of seek . . . study, examine thoroughly, penetrate, explore . . .

rarely reflects the true nature of our journey with God. In fact, it is not even close. Patrick Morley's quote from *Second Wind for the Second Half* is worth repeating:

> God talk runs high; God walk runs low. Why is that? As a culture we speak highly of God, but often as an enfeebled grandfather, appreciated for what he did in times past. It's not that we don't think highly of God—we do. We just don't think of him as relevant.

We do not value or seek that which we consider irrelevant. If we are to build our wall of personal spiritual growth, we must have a plan that guides us to walk the walk. We must have a heart and discipline for seeking the face of God. He must be real in our everyday lives. He must be relevant. We must discover, study, examine our souls, and explore the heart of the living God. We must embody the definition of *seek* in our spiritual walk.

If we are to accomplish our purpose in building a protective spiritual wall, we must have a process grounded in these key planning principles:

1. A commitment to spend quantity time in God's presence, and
2. A commitment to spiritually seek the heart of God.

The Process

Someone very insightful once said, "The road to hell is paved with good intentions." We all understand this good-intentions theory at a very personal level. As an example, most of us have purposed to read the Bible in its entirety, and many of you (I never got that far) bought the one-year Bible. January first was an exceptionally good day as we dove into the Scripture. Our personal commitment and spiritual energy level was high. Many of us survived the first month, and we lived to see God call Moses from the burning bush in Exodus. Most of us, intent on achieving our goal, never made it to March. All too often, our honorable, purposeful plans fall short. We fail to accomplish the desires of our hearts. We are disappointed. We dismiss our failed ventures into spiritual discipline as simply being beyond us, and we move on.

Our failures rarely reflect dishonorable purposes . . . quite the contrary. Our purpose is most often spiritually sound, and we have a workable plan in place to guide and assist us. Most often, we fall short due to a lack of personal discipline and the absence of a structured process to guide us. The swirling demands of our daily lives simply consume our calendars, and our journeys into God's arena fall by the wayside. The priorities of life displace our time with God.

You know the direction I am going. If you are reaching to slam on the brakes, I understand. If you are cringing at the very thought of a structured process, of disciplined handcuffs, you are in good company. Take a deep breath, and forge ahead with me. This is a critical part of our spiritual journey together. It is the very heartbeat of entering into the presence of God and growing to abide with Him.

There is absolutely no substitution for being in God's presence every day. There is no shortcut. There are two significant factors in play. This is both a spiritual and practical matter. First and foremost, we have clear spiritual direction from Jesus Himself. He said, " . . . take up [your] cross daily . . ." (Luke 9:23). He has spoken. He left no room for misinterpretation.

From a practical standpoint, we have all personally experienced the impact and value of consistency and discipline. A simple look at exercise is telling. It matters not whether we run alone in the morning or participate in a structured evening exercise program at the gym. If we exercise *every* Monday through Thursday, and we never miss a day, we are compelled to bounce out of bed at 5:00 A.M. on Wednesday to lace up the running shoes. We simply do not want to break our consistent routine. But, as we have all discovered, inconsistency has a rapid deteriorating effect. Once we miss a day or two, we tend to lose focus, and our commitment fades.

You may have had this same experience in dieting. The theory is identical. A big piece of chocolate cake on Saturday night has a way of undermining the very concept of dieting. A couple of juicy cheeseburgers, and we quickly drift back into our normal calorie-laden routine.

Exercising and dieting are great ideas. They have sound purpose. But as we have all experienced, if we do not have a bulletproof process to ensure consistency, our good intentions simply disappear. Growing into the presence of the living God, embracing His heart as the anchor for our souls, is no different. If we are to abide with Him, walk consistently in His path, and see His hand move in our midst, we must be there . . . every day. There is no other way.

As we have discovered, commitment to seeking the heart of God on a daily basis is the foundation of quantity time. Quantity time gives birth to quality time with God and a spiritually joyful relationship with Him. Spiritual joy frees the soul from the crippling pain of life and gives us rest in God's greater purpose. God's purpose gives us hope to face tomorrow. With heartfelt purpose and understanding, we strive forward and immerse ourselves in the process of spiritual discipline.

My recommended structure is grounded in the following five key principles. They embody the framework recommended by Bruce Wilkinson and others, and they incorporate my personal successes and failures over these past six-hundred-plus days.

1. Spend private time with God every day.
2. Choose a place of comfort.
3. Spiritual journaling is essential.
4. God's Word, God's Word, God's Word.
5. Independent spiritual journey.

My goal is to paint with a broad brush that establishes five foundational principles and leaves you the freedom to adapt them to your personal style and circumstances. This process is not an exact science. Your spiritual journey will be a learning experience. Over time, you will find your own spiritual path.

My next remark may surprise you, but it is heartfelt, and I believe it is sound spiritual advice. If you are not ready to embark on this disciplined spiritual journey of a lifetime . . . don't. I would highly recommend that you wait. I believe it would be counterproductive to begin this process if you truly believe that you are not ready. You may feel spiritually unprepared, or you may have circumstances in your life that would make it extremely difficult to begin such a journey at this time. Under such conditions, failure would be a virtual certainty, and an unsuccessful attempt would be disappointing. I would strongly encourage you to wait patiently, seek to walk in God's path daily, and prepare yourself spiritually. Search your heart . . . you will know when you are ready.

1. Spend private time with God every day.

- There is no substitution; developing a meaningful relationship with God is an everyday event.

- I strongly advise that you adapt your schedule to spend time with God in the morning. When I have failed to do so, I often find myself trying to work God into my schedule. I find that the process becomes obligatory in nature and tends to lack spiritual depth. I do not consider "mornings" to be an absolute. Your schedule and/or your style may dictate otherwise. Whatever you choose, be consistent.

2. Choose a place of comfort.

- Find a place where you are at peace, a place where you can feel His very presence. Emotional and spiritual solitude is critical.

- You must be in a place that allows you to get lost in His Word. A deep walk with God is an absolute must if you are to sense His presence in Scripture.

- I found the coffee shop to be joyful and very productive initially . . . but my time there evolved into something of a ministry in and of itself. Eventually, I had to find private time elsewhere to attain that place of solitude.

- You may find it necessary to be absolutely alone.

3. Spiritual journaling is essential.

- Spiritual journaling is not a personal diary. It is not a reflection of how your day is going.

- As Wilkinson states, it is not a stab at literary work. It simply reflects your spiritual heartbeat, your day-to-day spiritual journey. I have often been asked what I routinely write in my journal. The following excerpt is representative of my daily journaling:

April 2nd, 2003 [493] Deep spiritual journey in Isaiah. Deep, deep into Isaiah. Chapter 53—*the Lord's will to "crush him and cause him to suffer"* in order that many be justified; that he bear their iniquities. After the suffering of his soul . . . he will see the light of life . . . the ultimate Painful Gift. Take a deep breath this morning, and rest in Him. Place both hands on the arm of God, hold on, don't let go. As circumstances seem dark, and the light of the world dims, *trust and rely.*

- I have found it to be a powerful emotional tool. Recording my one-year anniversary (November 25, 2002 [365]) was both joyful and inspiring. Those who have followed in my path display the same excitement about numerical milestones.
- When your day simply gets away from you and you do not have your regular thirty minutes or an hour, a simple entry into the spiritual journal maintains consistency and protects from "exercise/diet" drift. Over the course of my six-hundred-plus days, I have had three or four such experiences. They lack spiritual depth for the day in question, but they protect the journey.

- Joyfully, I have not experienced a spiritual "lull" during my journey. But I am certain that I will face it. I believe that the journaling process will be my anchor of commitment and consistency when I am otherwise adrift.

4. *God's Word, God's Word, God's Word.*
- Spend time in the Bible every day.
- I grew to experience God's presence in His Word. I allowed myself to get lost in Scripture. Some mornings it may take fifteen or twenty minutes to isolate yourself from the world and find that level of spiritual depth, but there is no substitution.
- Sound spiritual literature is a great adjunct to the Bible, but it is not a replacement. Too often, we leave the Bible on the shelf.
- I have opted to study the Bible every day—straight through. As I shared earlier, I finished Revelation one day and started Genesis again the next day. I intend to do that forever—but I don't think my style is for everyone. I strongly suggest that you consider a daily study guide. It may give you more balance and keep you on track. The following study guides have been recommended and are worthy of your consideration:

1. *My Utmost for His Highest*—Chambers
2. *Streams in the Desert*—Cowman
3. *Daily Light*—Lotz

- Choose a course of study that gives you consistent spiritual energy.

5. *Independent spiritual journey.*
   - Be alone with God.
   - I am in no way discouraging studying God's Word with your spouse or in an accountability group. However, I believe long-term personal spiritual growth requires committed time with just you and God. In that in-depth time alone, He speaks.

To experience the hope that God has so richly promised, we must embrace the loving, living God on a full-time basis. Building a spiritual wall, the transformation of the heart, is not a magical euphoric mountaintop experience.

Abiding with Christ
is achieved through a systematic process,
grounded in seeking God's presence on a consistent basis,
with a personal commitment to His greater purpose.
We are breaking the basic human nature of self-will
with spiritual disciplines.

We do not leave our spiritual journey to chance. We do not go the route of the lone ranger. We do not leave ourselves vulnerable to the emotional roller coaster of circumstances. God becomes the epicenter of our very spiritual existence, and the paralyzing pain of life is reduced to an instrument of His purpose. We build a wall. We empower God in our everyday lives. We make Him relevant. We put Him first.

We experience spiritual revolution. In the words of Dallas Willard, it is a "revolution of character." His book, *Renovation of the Heart*, speaks to the essence of our spiritual journey. "We change from the inside out through an ongoing personal relationship to God in Christ. It changes our ideas, beliefs, feelings, and habits of choice, as well as our bodily tendencies and social relations. *It penetrates to the deepest layers of our soul.*"

God's living presence in our lives reaches beyond our attitudes and actions, and touches our character and the deepest desires of our hearts. We are being transformed into His likeness. We have begun the spiritual journey of a lifetime. We build . . . we build every day. We build to ensure that we are forever grounded in His living word, are walking consistently in His path, are protected by His merciful hand, and are growing to be living instruments for His purpose.

His Purpose

"As he went along, he saw a man blind from birth.
His disciples asked him,
'Rabbi, who sinned, this man or his parents, that he was born blind?'
'Neither this man nor his parents sinned,' said Jesus,
'but this happened so that the work of God
might be displayed in his life.'"
—*John 9:1–3*

As we continue with the Spiritual Cycle, we do so with newfound insight. We have stepped beyond our spiritual rules and regulations and into the heart, the very essence of the living God. We are building daily, building a wall of spiritual strength, seeking to abide in the heart of God. We seek to know His perfect will. The spiritual truth of abiding with the living God takes precedence over all circumstances. We walk in God's path. Life's painful circumstances do not disappear. In fact, looking again at figure 9 of the Spiritual Cycle reveals that "bad" circumstances are ever-present regardless of the status of our relationship with God. But now, walking in the light, we look upon life's tragedies with the certainty of God's presence, a heart for His purpose, and His promise of hope.

The blackened tree trunks stand like charred wooden gravestones.
The smoke-filled haze hovers lifelessly just above the earth's surface.
The silence is deafening, the stillness eerie.

The raging forest fire, driven by gale-force winds
swept through at lightning speed leaving total destruction in its path.
In the midst of the screaming, roaring blaze,
firefighters struggled in desperation,
seeking to save the forest and themselves.

They now sit in silence,
black sweat dripping from their chiseled, charcoal-smudged faces.
As they stare blindly into the distance, there is no evidence of life.
What once was . . . is no more.

It is over. The sun is setting.
We cannot fathom that it could possibly rise again.

Though circumstances make it seem impossible, we now know for certain that God's hand is present. He is always present. God's Word brings comfort and gives light where there is darkness. He

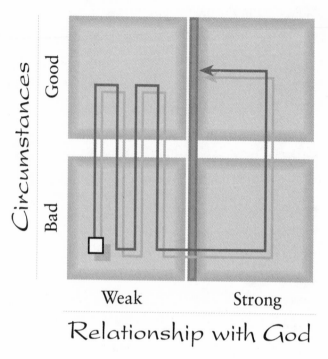

Fig. 9.

speaks in the midst of the intense heat and from the stillness of night:

> There is a time for everything,
> and a season for every activity under heaven:
> a time to be born and a time to die,
> a time to plant and a time to uproot,
> a time to kill and a time to heal,
> a time to tear down and a time to build,
> a time to weep and a time to laugh,
> a time to mourn and a time to dance,
> a time to scatter stones and a time to gather them,
> a time to embrace and a time to refrain,
> a time to search and a time to give up,

a time to keep and a time to throw away,

a time to tear and a time to mend,

a time to be silent and a time to speak,

a time to love and a time to hate,

a time for war and a time for peace (Eccl. 3:1–8).

There is a time for the blazing, crippling forest fire of life. Over time, the vines had climbed high into the treetops, bringing darkness upon the forest, preventing growth and damaging existing foliage. Simultaneously, the thorny briers flourished and covered the forest floor, suffocating any hope of new life. Now, the fires have come . . . and gone. The suffocating overgrowth is no more. God's creation is free . . . free to breathe again. God has spoken. He has made Himself known. Such is the nature of God's hand in our lives.

For we know that in the devastation of the raging fire, God is at work. He acts with purpose. We see devastation; God sees opportunity. It is a matter of perspective. God's majestic strength emerges, made perfect in our weakness. Our pain gives opportunity for God to rescue us, to teach us, and to lift us up in His love.

The prophet Jeremiah experienced this firsthand. Devastated at his life crumbling around him, he pleaded with the Lord for understanding: Why did you ever allow my mother to give birth to a man who would face such strife and contention? I have done nothing wrong, but everyone curses me.

The Lord saw his pain and heard his cry for help. With these powerful words, He gave Jeremiah hope:

Surely, I will deliver you for a good purpose . . . in times of disaster and times of distress (Jer. 15:11).

As Jeremiah personally experienced, devastation gives way to rebirth. God's greater purpose, His gift of hope, is born in the heart of pain. This is the truth of God's Word and His heart.

Our family experienced God's promise. His love and His purpose were displayed in living color in our personal journey. In my sinfulness, in my weakness, His strength was made known. God displayed His perfect heart and will. In my spiritual rebirth, He flooded our home with His love and grace. God's purpose, His eternal purpose, came to life. Jeannie and I witnessed God's miraculous hand as He spoke to our hearts in His still, small voice. We embraced Him. We fell in love again.

Each of the beautiful children that God has entrusted us with would come to know with certainty that God works miracles. The valley of the shadow of death had disappeared in their very presence. The impossible had happened, and they had lived it.

My love for God's Word gave wings to spiritual renewal in the hearts of family and friends from South Carolina to Arizona—His miraculous multiplication at work. Through my weakness, God's strength was made evident, and He lifted the pens of a number of men and women across America to spend time in His Word and journal every day.

And I will not forget the little girl who cried alone in her daddy's empty closet. She had expressed her emotional devastation in the poem, "Overload." She had asked the very question of whether or not it was worth fighting the battle. She would breathe spiritual oxygen, and write again. Her heart, in a revelation of God's presence, speaks:

God's Grace

You always hear people say
you can feel God's presence.
But for some unknown reason
you never thought it made sense.

Could you have imagined then
what you would see today.
Because God let you see himself
in a completely different way.

Speaking with a stranger
as if you'd known them all your life
Relating to them deeply
even if they don't seem like your type.

Throughout the conversation
you gaze into their face
And suddenly it hits you
they're covered in God's grace.

Isn't it amazing
the things you're being shown
And suddenly you understand
everything you thought you'd known.

You want to shout with glory
as if they aren't aware
That you see God's love in them
and you're thankful that they're willing to share.

Our daughter, in overload, survived and lived to see people "covered in God's grace." In her youthful heart, she experienced God's miraculous hand. She saw His eternal purpose. She lived it.

Our walk with God takes precedence over life's circumstances, and our perspective changes. The forest fires are no less prevalent, but we see beyond the roaring flames and the billowing smoke. They now represent life, not death. The painful circumstances of life represent the beginning, not the end.

And the Beat Goes On

Difficult circumstances are not a once-in-a-lifetime event. They are ever-present in our lives. We do not grow beyond them. We do not solve them. We do not put them behind us as a distant memory. A heartfelt acceptance of difficult circumstances in life is instrumental to our spiritual peace, growing into God's presence. It is a learning process. It reflects our spiritual maturity.

Paul, a great man of God, lived and learned this spiritual truth. He went from the persecutor to the persecuted, from the highest mountaintop to the deepest valley, from a face-to-face meeting with Jesus on the road to Damascus . . . to prison. Paul came to delight in his imprisonment, his weakness. When he was weak, "Christ's power" rested on him (2 Cor. 12:9). Paul grew to follow, to walk in God's path, and to cherish God speaking through him. And in so doing, he "learned to be content whatever the circumstances." He knew what it meant to have plenty and he knew what it meant to be needy. He learned the secret of being content in every situation. In the midst of persecution and prison, he grew to understand that he could survive anything and accomplish all that God placed before him through the strength that God had given him (Phil. 4:11–12). In the midst of his own living hell, Paul rejoiced always (2 Cor. 6:10). He displayed God's heart to those who imprisoned him and he continued to minister by writing letters to the churches he founded. He became prayerful and thankful in everything. The prison cell could not paralyze his heart. In chains, God rested in his soul. Paul knew what it meant to be a follower.

Paul's banner, "contentment in all things," is critical to our walk in God's path. We have seen that God's hand is present at all times. He is constantly at work . . . for His purpose. In the fifty-fifth chapter of Isaiah, God gives us assurance that His Word will not return empty. It will accomplish His desire, His eternal purpose. We have His promise.

This is the very heart of *Painful Gifts*. In the midst of the forest fire, life's horrific pain, God makes His heart known. It is a time for rebirth. We see it in His Word and we experience it in our lives. Again and again, we are challenged to grow into God's presence, understand His very nature, and be living instruments for His purpose.

- We are challenged in order that we grow to rely on Him.

  . . . We were under great pressure, far beyond our ability to endure, so that we despaired even of life. Indeed, in our hearts we felt the sentence of death. But this happened that we might not rely on ourselves but on God . . . (2 Cor. 1:8–9).

- We are challenged in order that our hearts remain humble.

To keep me from becoming conceited . . . there was given me a thorn in my flesh . . . (2 Cor. 12:7).

- We are challenged in order that our capacity to share His love might grow.

Praise be to the God and Father of our Lord Jesus Christ, the Father of compassion and . . . comfort, who comforts us in all our troubles, so that we can comfort those in any trouble with the comfort we ourselves have received from God . . . through Christ our comfort overflows (2 Cor. 1:3–5).

- We are challenged to make way for God's perfection . . . His perfect presence in us.

. . . My grace is sufficient for you, for my power is made perfect in weakness . . . (2 Cor. 12:9).

We are on the road to Damascus with Paul. We are in prison with him. We find strength as "Christ's power . . . rest[s] on [us]," as God Himself "transcends all understanding . . . guard[s] [our] hearts and [our] minds . . ." (2 Cor. 12:9, Phil. 4:7). We, like Moses, persevere because we, in faith, grow to see Him who is invisible. We have entered into God's realm and we rest in His power.

Let's embrace God's challenge. Let's fix our eyes on Jesus, the architect of our journey, and run with perseverance the race before us (Heb. 12:1–3). Let's listen carefully to Jesus as He challenges us. He is speaking directly to us, "I have . . . appoint[ed] you as a servant and . . . witness of what you have seen of me and what I will show you" (Acts 26:16). We have been to the valley of the shadow of death; we have stood in silence and disbelief as life's forest fires raged; and we have survived to see Him. He has emerged to paint a picture of perfection . . . His strength in our weakness. In our painful emptiness, He has proven Himself to be the miraculous giver of joyful gifts . . . the gifts of grace and hope. The gifts are ours. They are gifts of the heart. God has passed us the baton. His perfect presence is in us. Let's run the race.

Run the Race

"Why does the way of the wicked prosper?
Why do all the faithless live at ease?
You have planted them,
and they have taken root;
they grow and bear fruit.
You are always on their lips
but far from their hearts. . . .
Drag them off like sheep to be butchered!"
—Jeremiah 12:1–3

The above verses are Jeremiah's complaint. God answered:

If you have raced with men on foot
and they have worn you out,
how can you compete with horses?
If you stumble in safe country,
how will you manage
in the thickets by the Jordan? (Jer. 12:5).

For a lifetime, we raced with the men on foot and they wore us out. We went alone and, we, like Jeremiah, asked, "Why? Why? Why?" The painful circumstances of life were crippling. But we survived. We did more than just survive. We lived to see the person of God and receive His gift of hope. Because we have grasped the truth, abiding in the presence of the living God (in the Spiritual Cycle), we can run with the horses. We can face the thickets by the Jordan because we are not alone. We can run the race . . . and we must. God has called us for His greater purpose.

I have vivid recollection of sitting in my dad's hospital room the night before he had open-heart surgery. It was a powerful moment. Having suffered a near-fatal heart attack, he, well into his seventies, was sharing his heart with our family . . . perhaps for the last time. He knew it. Everyone in the room knew it. He reminisced, expressing deep appreciation for his family and, in particular, his love for my mother. He held her hand warmly. He patted her leg. With no way of knowing that he would miraculously survive an eleventh-hour setback, he wanted to imprint his love on our hearts with his final words, creating an image that would last for a lifetime. He wanted us to be absolutely certain of his love . . . he wanted us to never forget.

So is the heart of Jesus as He speaks to His disciples, beginning in the thirteenth chapter of John:

> It was just before the Passover Feast. Jesus knew that the time had come for him to leave this world and go to the Father. Having loved his own who were in the world, *he now showed them the full extent of his love* (v. 1).

Jesus knew that His time on earth was coming to an end. Just as my father sought to imprint his everlasting love on the hearts of his family, Jesus would extend His heart to His apostles in order that they might fully understand His message, know the depth of His love, and be encouraged and strengthened.

In their final hours together, Jesus searched the eager but stunned, confused faces of His apostles and He told them, "This is to my Father's glory, that you bear much fruit, showing yourselves to be my disciples" (John 15:8). As the hour grew late, Jesus looked into the eyes of His apostles and He challenged them to embrace God's greater purpose. He directed them to bear spiritual fruit, and in so doing, reveal their hearts of discipleship. During His ministry on earth, Jesus taught them to race with the footmen. In the eighth verse, He challenges them to run with the horses . . . to run the race.

We, like His twelve apostles, have grasped the living presence of God, and we are bolstered by His message. We are challenged to walk in His path, embrace His greater purpose, and live lives of spiritual fruitfulness.

The Spiritual Cycle, as depicted in figure 10, displays the direct correlation between our relationship with God and spiritual fruit. A strong relationship with God embodies the very heart of abiding with Him and results in the consistent outpouring of "much" fruit. Not surprisingly, the impact of life's circumstances has been diminished. Circumstances no longer dominate our thoughts and our actions. "Much" spiritual fruit is realized equally during both good and bad circumstances. We are not surprised, for we have learned that our internal strength, our spiritual fortitude, is not circumstance dependent. Jesus said so:

. . . If a man remains *in me* and I *in him, he will* bear much fruit; apart from me you can do nothing (John 15:5).

We have discovered "our source of power and protection all the time." *In Him,* resting behind our protective spiritual wall, *we will* bear much fruit because His power is made perfect in us. Producing spiritual fruit, God's prize for running the race is pure joy.

The concept of spiritual fruit is often misunderstood and misconstrued. We primarily view spiritual fruit as good works, and it embodies the negative connotation of "obligation." Our minds instantly think of the church's insatiable need for teachers in the nursery, counselors for the summer youth trip, and an active outreach program—we instantly throw on the internal emotional brakes!

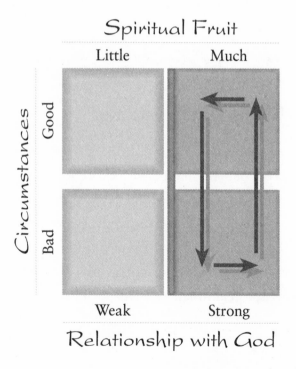

Fig. 10.

Nothing could be further from the truth. Spiritual fruit is not a scheduled, obligatory event. Spiritual fruit is not found in a laundry list of our church commitments. The concept of fruit is an inward spiritual experience, a personal journey "in Him" that joyfully penetrates our innermost beings. I like to think of it simply as spiritual oxygen. God's continued presence, that which we live and breathe, is revealed in us inwardly (our character), outwardly (our day-to-day behavior), and in our complete being (the heart and mind).

As we run the race, we grow in spirit, protected by the never-ending construction of our spiritual wall. Inwardly, we grow to reflect the character of our leader, Jesus Himself. We build every day and we grow to embody the fruit of the Spirit:

> . . . love, joy, peace, patience, kindness, goodness, faithfulness, gentleness and self-control . . . (Gal. 5:22–23).

It is neither purposeful nor obligatory. We simply inhale and we exhale. One breath at a time, we take on the character and person of God. "Since we live by the Spirit, let us keep in step with the Spirit" (Gal. 5:25).

As we walk in His path and "keep in step with the Spirit," our outward behavior evolves to reflect our innermost beings. Neither overt commitment nor long-term planning is needed. Our actions reveal our hearts. God, the cheerful giver, "is able to make all grace abound to [us], so that in all things at all times, having all that [we] need, [we] will abound in every good work" (2 Cor. 9:8). We live and breathe God's purpose as we abide "in Him." Our commitment to His purpose no longer reflects "what we do"; it is an image of "who we are."

We have arrived at the spiritual mountaintop. We understand what it means to abide in His presence, to be complete in Him, to be transformed. Paul speaks in the twelfth chapter of Romans. As we experience transformation, the renewing of the mind, *then* we "will be able to test and approve what God's will is—His good, pleasing, and perfect will" (v. 2).

We follow the Leader and we are transformed into His likeness.

Our light shines brightly. Men "see [our] good deeds and praise [our] Father in heaven . . ." (Matt. 5:16).

We "remain in [His] love" (John 15:9), we grasp the baton, God's gift of hope, and we run the race . . . we run with the horses.

The Power of Hope

*"May the God of hope fill you
with all joy and peace
as you trust in him, so that
you may overflow with hope
by the power of the Holy Spirit."*
—Romans 15:13

As the days passed, Tracie and I would sit face-to-face at the small round table. She would sit solemnly, she would laugh, she would tear up, and she would joke around. She was consumed with the full spectrum of emotions, clouding her ability to think. She wanted me to give her the right answer, but I could not. I did not have it. The answer would come from within her soul. She would have to find it.

She would burst through the door, sit down, and declare that she was going to have an abortion . . . end of discussion. Fifteen minutes later she would drop her chin, stare mindlessly at the table, and sadly declare that she simply could not abort her unborn child. The sand was slipping silently through the hourglass. She was running out of time.

Then, without fanfare, she walked in and sat down peacefully one morning. The anxiety that had consumed her for weeks was gone. Her face was relaxed, her smile soft. Her sky-blue eyes, the very same eyes that had initially searched for acceptance, now glistened with joy. She looked at me, brimming with confidence, and told me that she had made a decision—a final decision—to have her baby.

She did not speak with naïveté. She spoke with great clarity, mapping out the challenges that she would face. But, in the end, circumstances, the difficult challenges of life, had not been her guide, her internal compass.

She had searched inwardly, seeking God's presence, and found contentment. There is a beautiful moment here that we should not miss. In the end, Tracie and I did not place the pro-choice/pro-life issue on that little round table and arm-wrestle over it. No, she did not make her decision under the cloud of guilt. She searched and found hope in God's presence; an anchor for her soul, firm and secure.

In the words of my Russian friend, Genady Prutianov, I say, "Praise God."

Selected Bibliography

Chambers, Oswald. *My Utmost for His Highest*. New York, N.Y.: Dodd, Meade & Co., 1935.

Collins, Jim. *Good to Great: Why Some Companies Make the Leap . . . And Others Don't*. New York, N.Y.: HarperCollins Publishers, Inc., 2001.

Cowman, Mrs. Charles E. *Streams in the Desert: 366 Daily Devotional Readings*. Los Angeles, Calif.: The Oriental Mission Society, 1925.

Foster, Richard. *Celebration of Discipline: The Path to Spiritual Growth*. New York, N.Y.: Harper & Row, 1978.

Lotz, Anne Graham. *Daily Light Devotional*. Nashville, Tenn.: W Publishing Group, 1998.

Moen, Don. *God Will Make a Way: The Best of Don Moen*. Integrity's Hosanna! Music, 1990.

Morley, Patrick. *Second Wind for the Second Half*. Grand Rapids, Mich.: Zondervan Publishing House, 1999.

Wilkinson, Bruce H. *The Prayer of Jabez: Breaking Through to the Blessed Life*. Sisters, Ore.: Multnomah Publishers, Inc., 2000.

———— *Secrets of the Vine: Breaking Through to Abundance*. Sisters, Ore.: Multnomah Publishers, Inc., 2001.

Willard, Dallas. *Renovation of the Heart: Putting on the Character of Christ*. Colorado Springs, Colo.: NavPress Publishing Group, 2002.

Yancey, Philip. *What's So Amazing About Grace?* Grand Rapids, Mich.: Zondervan Publishing House, 1997.

About the Author

A native of Macon, Georgia, Dewey Greene earned his bachelor's degree in engineering from Georgia Tech and received a master's degree in health-care administration from Duke University in 1979. He served as CEO at several hospitals during his early career, including Decatur Hospital in Atlanta, Georgia; Trinity Medical Center in Dallas, Texas; and Longview Regional Hospital in Longview, Texas. In the mid-1990s, Greene was appointed division president for HCA, where he was responsible for thirteen hospitals in a tri-state regional area. He now serves as a consultant to the health-care industry.

Greene resides in Nashville, Tennessee, with Jeannie, his wife of twenty-eight years. They are the parents of four daughters and one son. *Painful Gifts* is his first book.

To order additional copies of *Painful Gifts*,
visit www.painfulgifts.com.
